Gingko Press

Still Lifes, U.S.A.

When I'm out and around shooting pictures, sometimes people approach me. They want to know what I'm doing in their neighborhood or on their property. They tell me they're concerned that I'm casing their house, or they think I'm with a government agency or insurance company looking for evidence of some sort. They're suspicious because I'm usually photographing mundane subjects and they can not imagine what I'm attracted to. If I'm a real photographer why not photograph nice stuff, they ask. My first instinct is to tell them that I'm an artist, hoping this will relieve their concerns. This rarely works, and they often tell me I don't look like an artist. So then I try to explain exactly what I'm doing. By their puzzled looks I know that doesn't convince them either. At a loss, I change the subject and tell them I'm from Holland. Somehow that seems to defuse them, and it gets me off the hook.

Rudy VanderLans

Astoria, New York

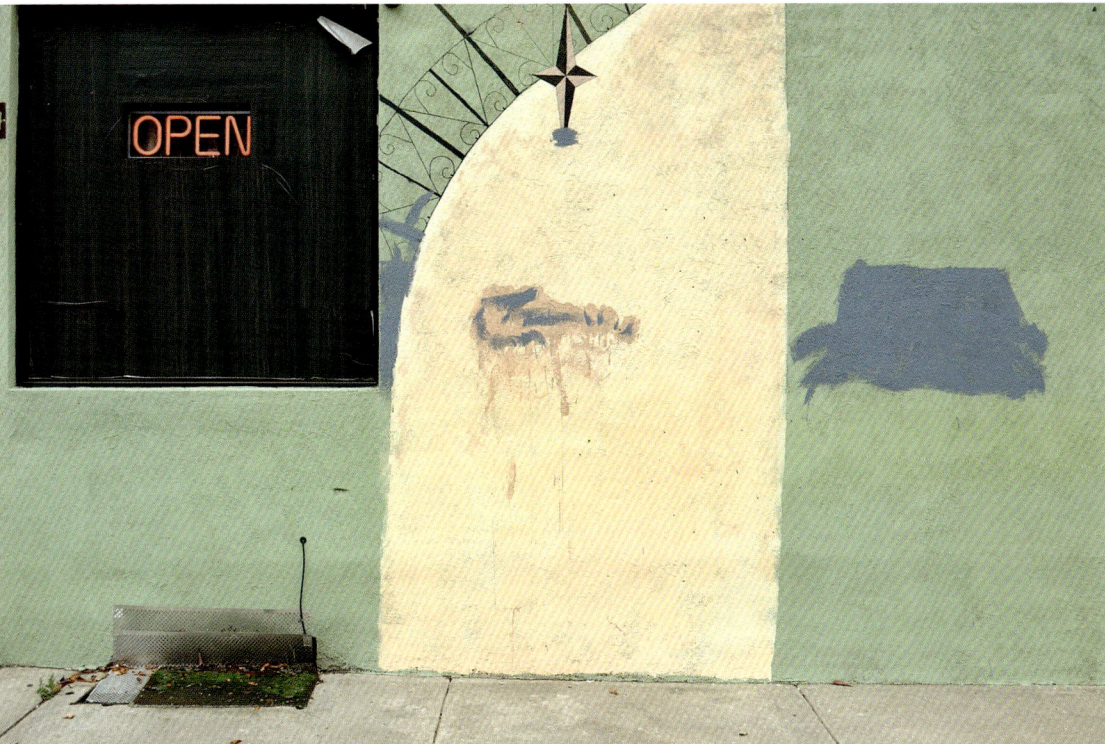

Detroit, Michigan

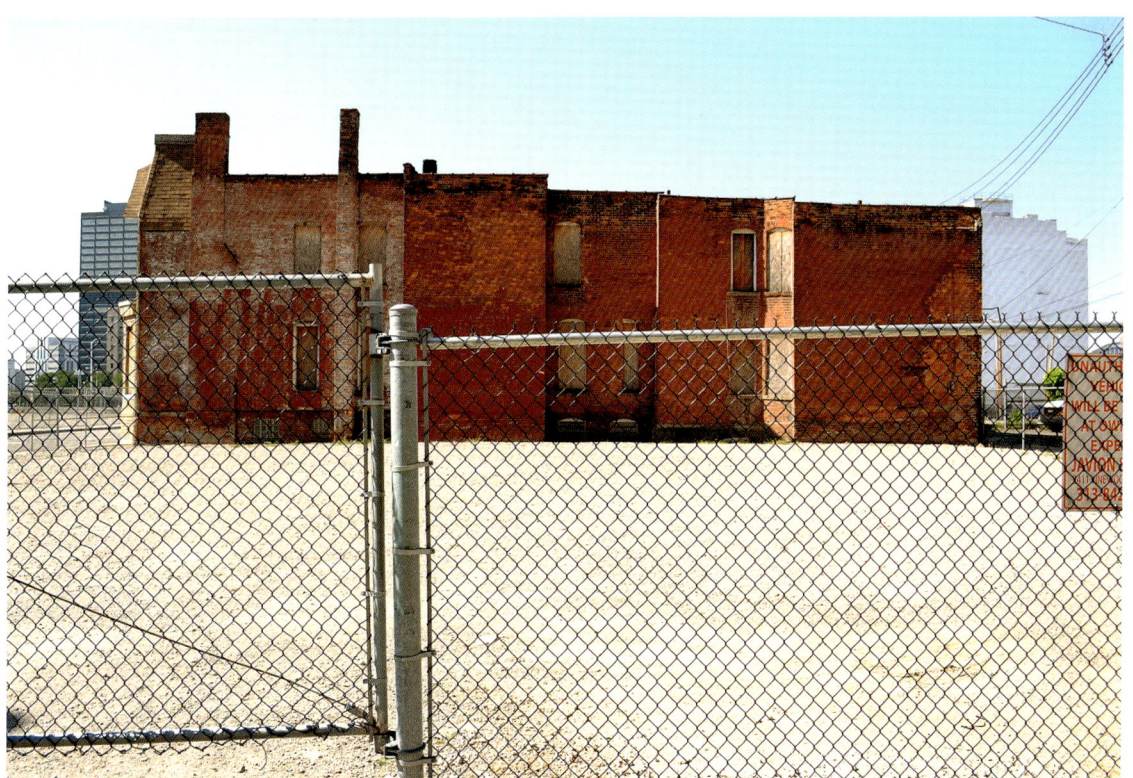

Arcadia, California

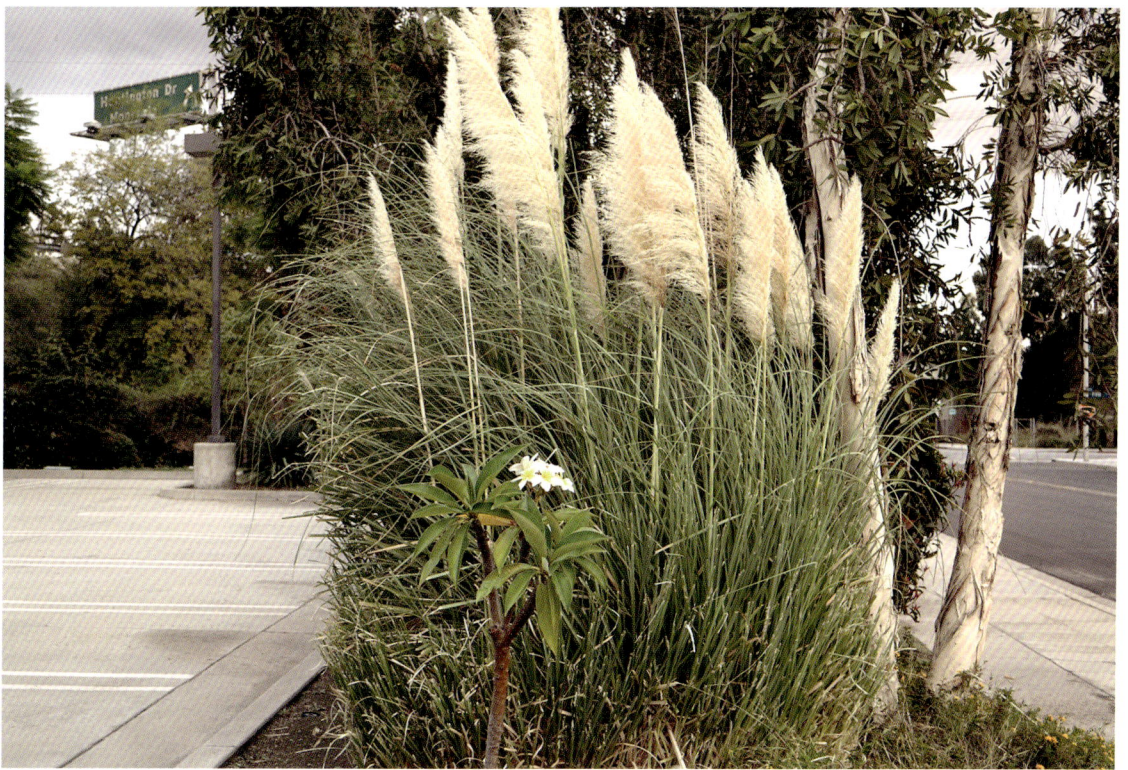

Cañon City, Colorado

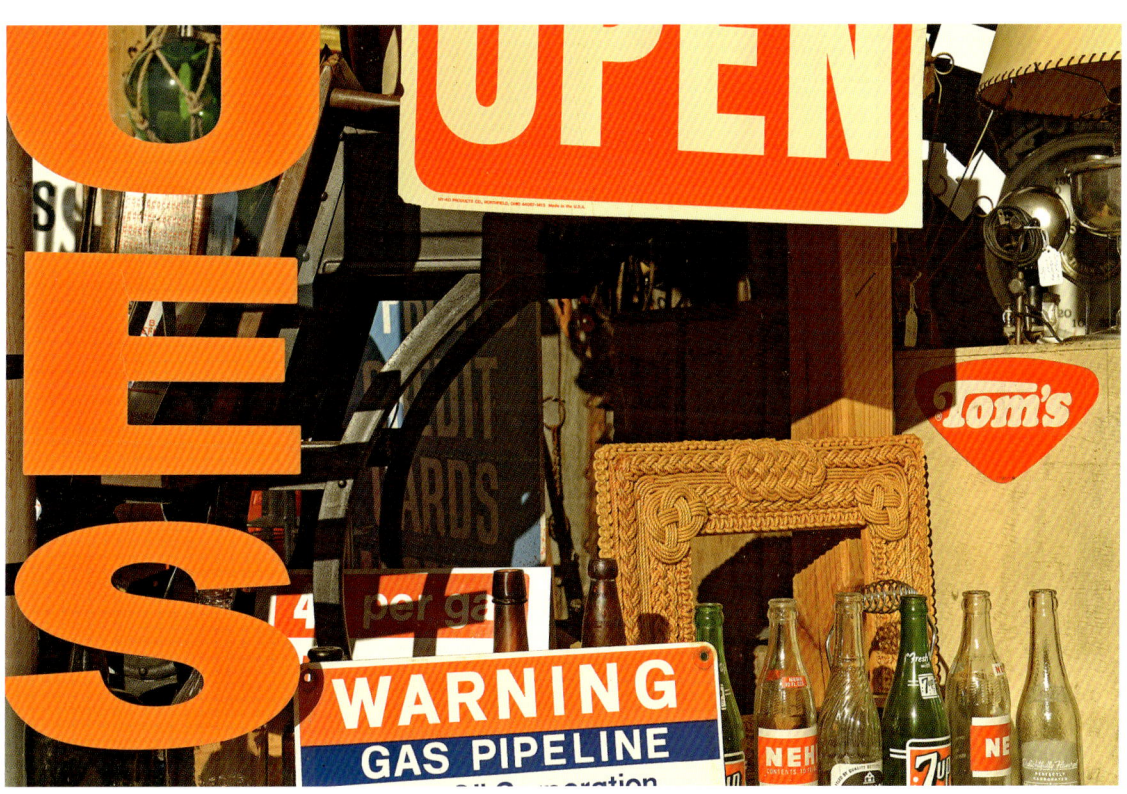

Kansas City, Missouri

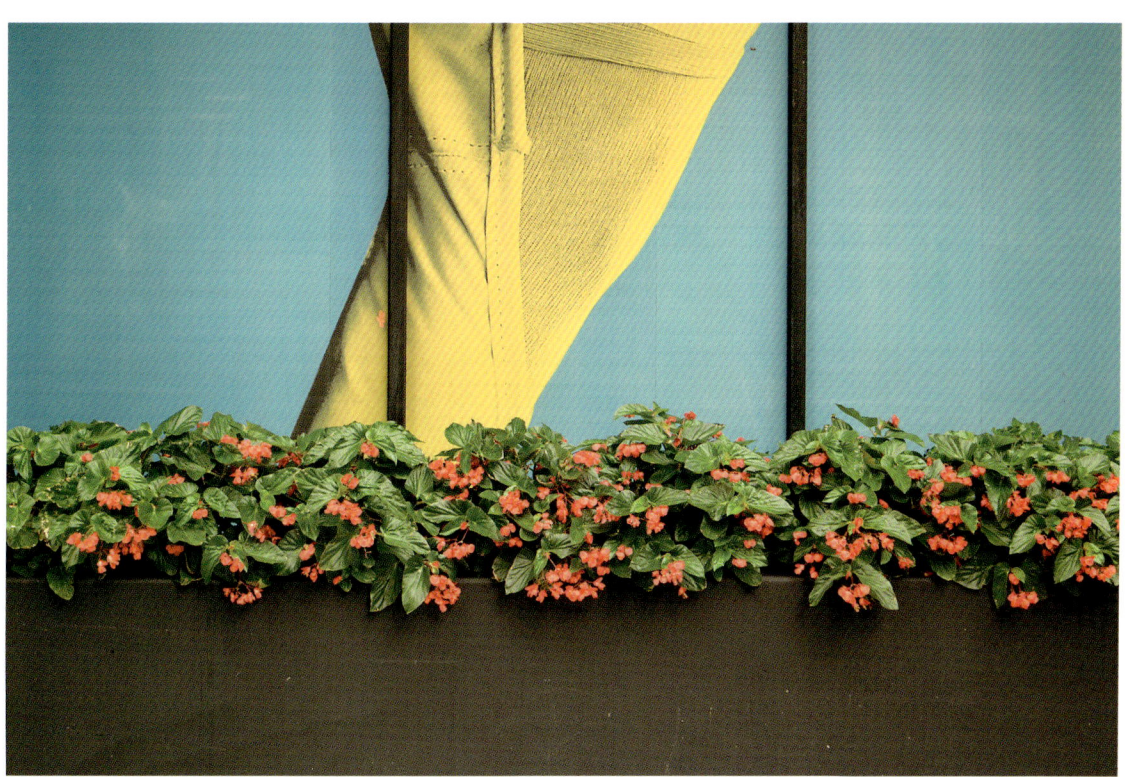

Atchison, Kansas

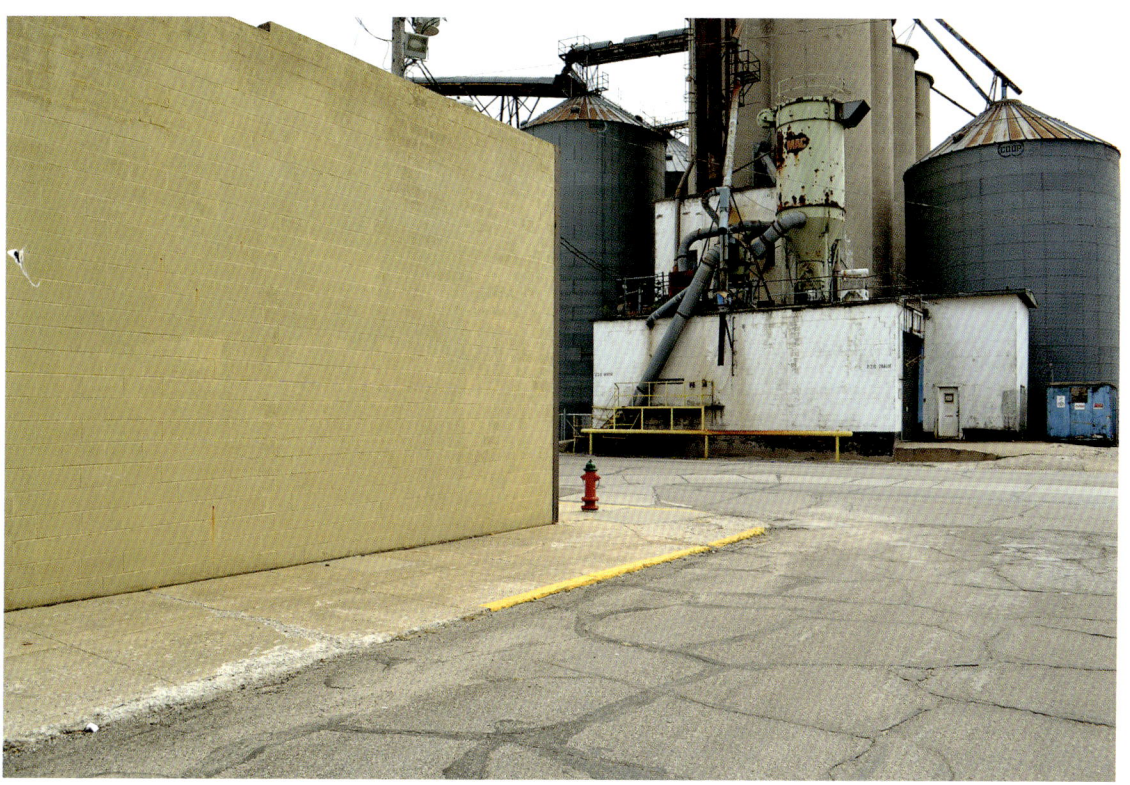

The Bronx, New York

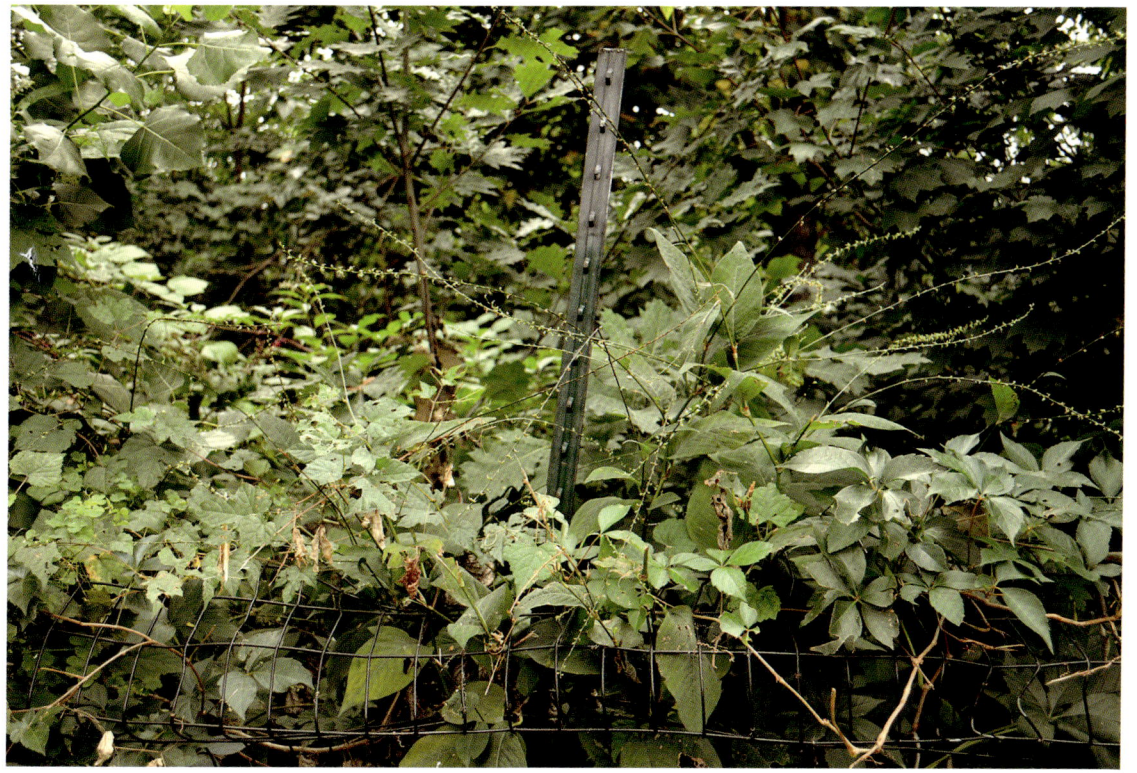

St. Joseph, Missouri

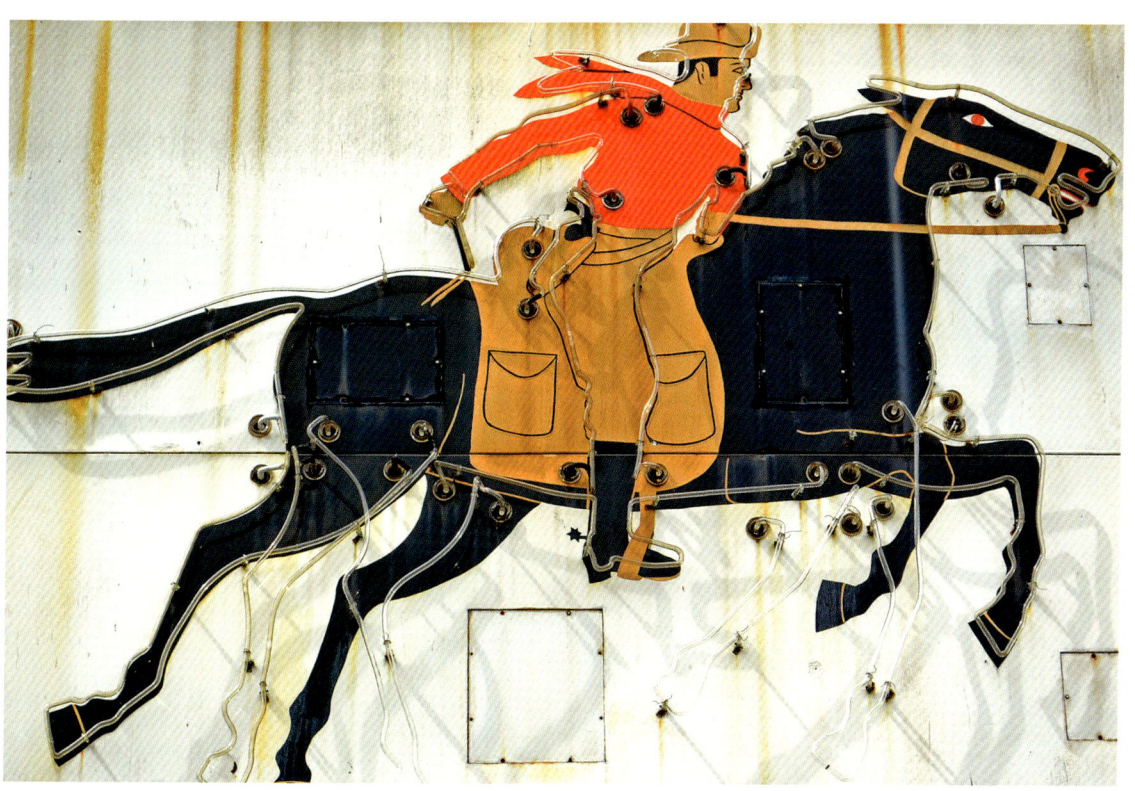

Bunker Hill, Kansas

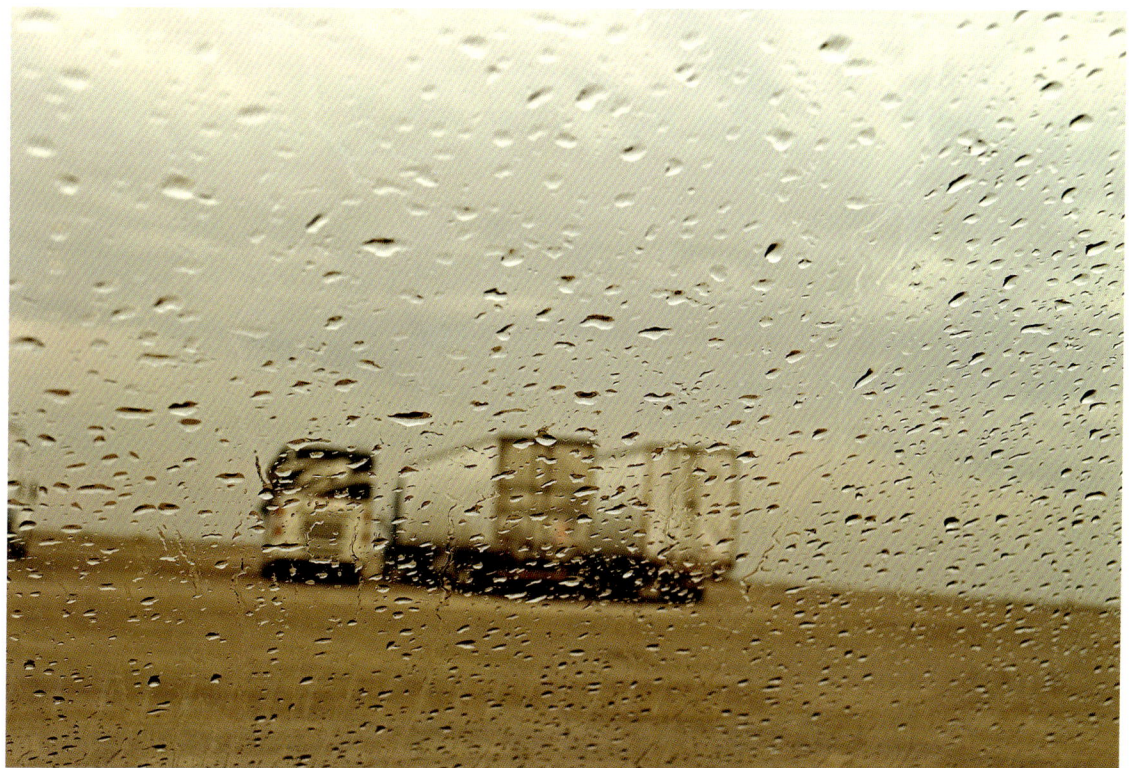

Kingman, Arizona

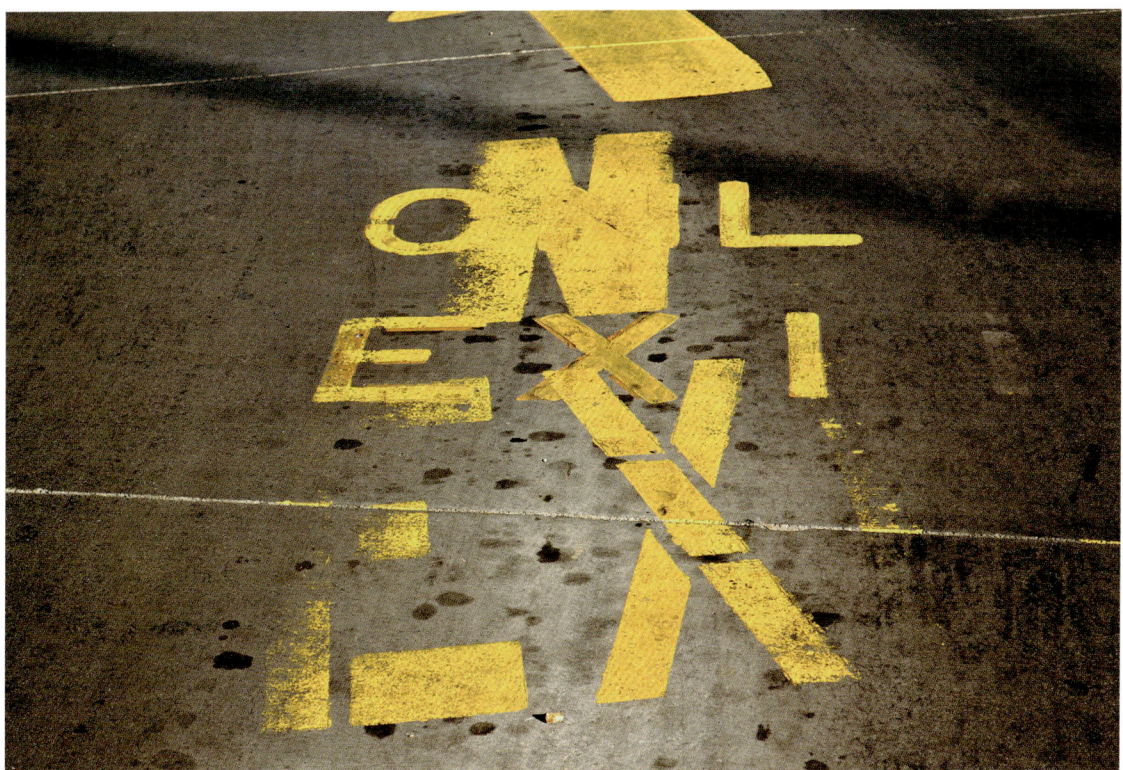

Primm, Nevada

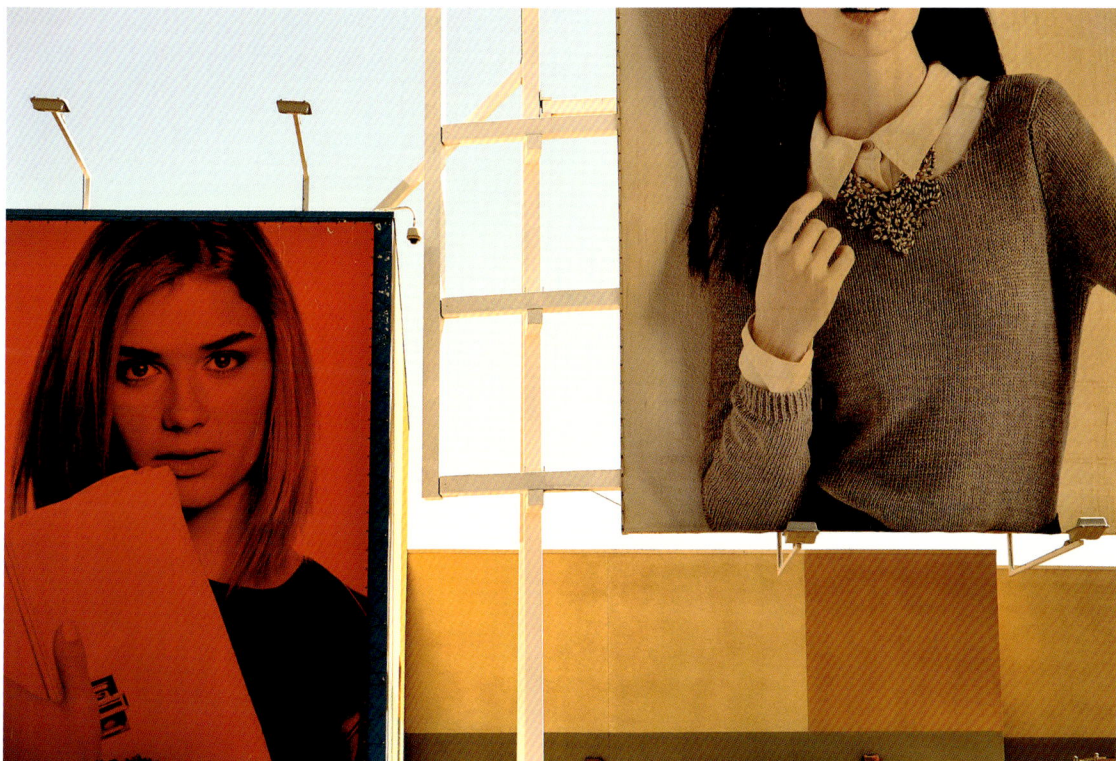

Kit Carson County, Colorado

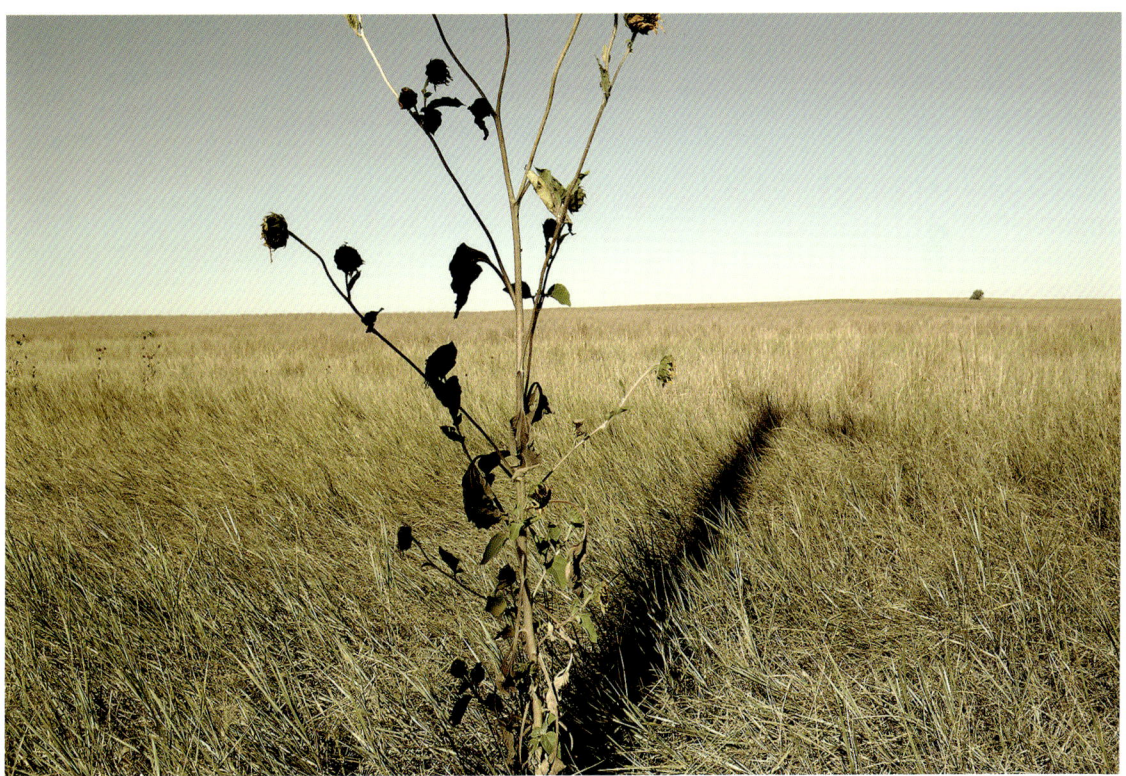

Astoria, New York

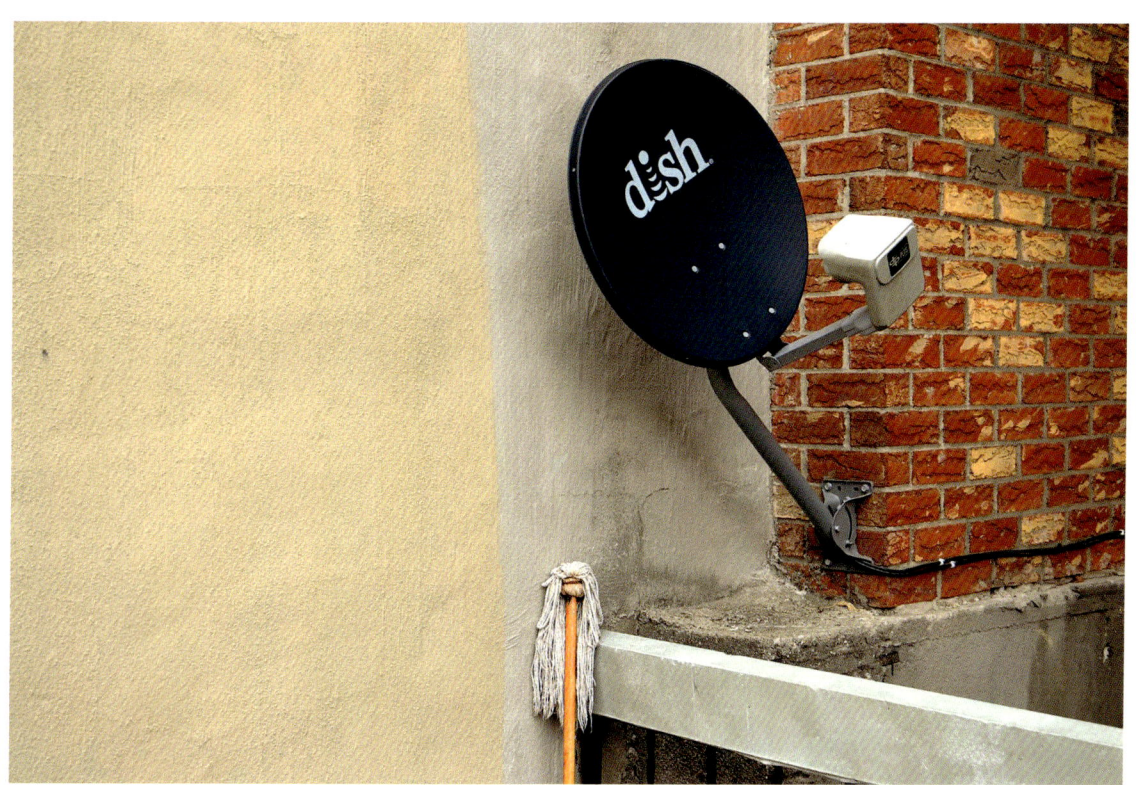

Farmington, New Mexico

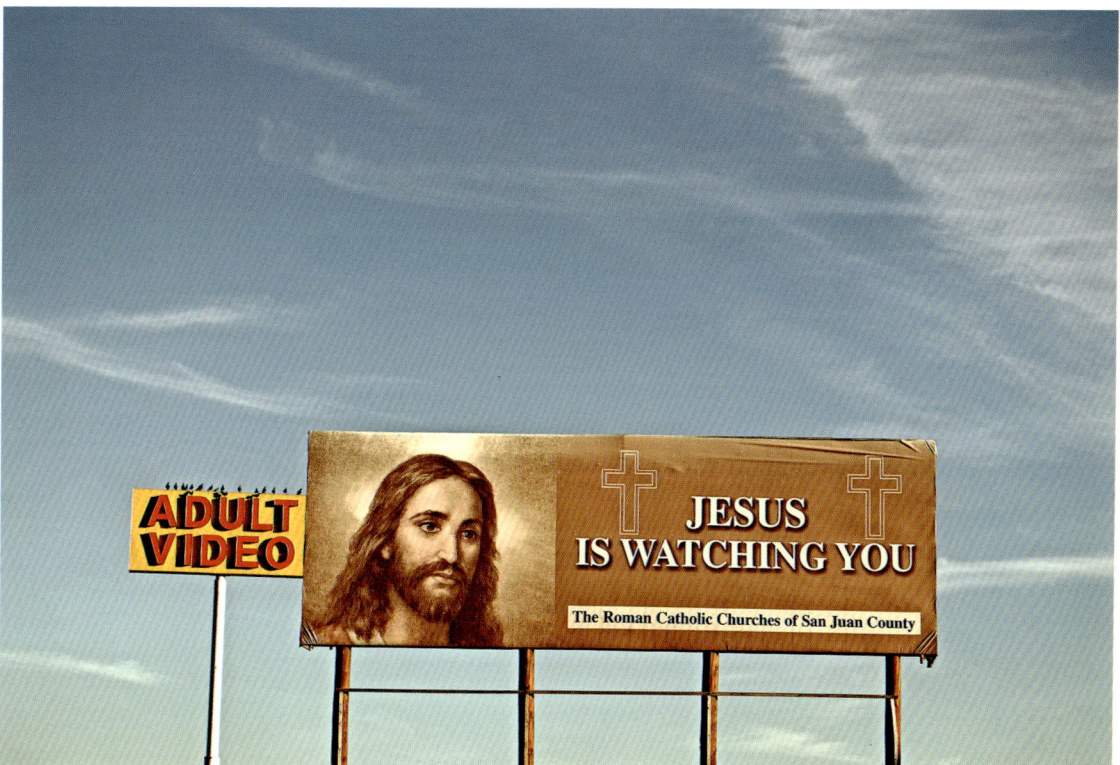

California, Missouri

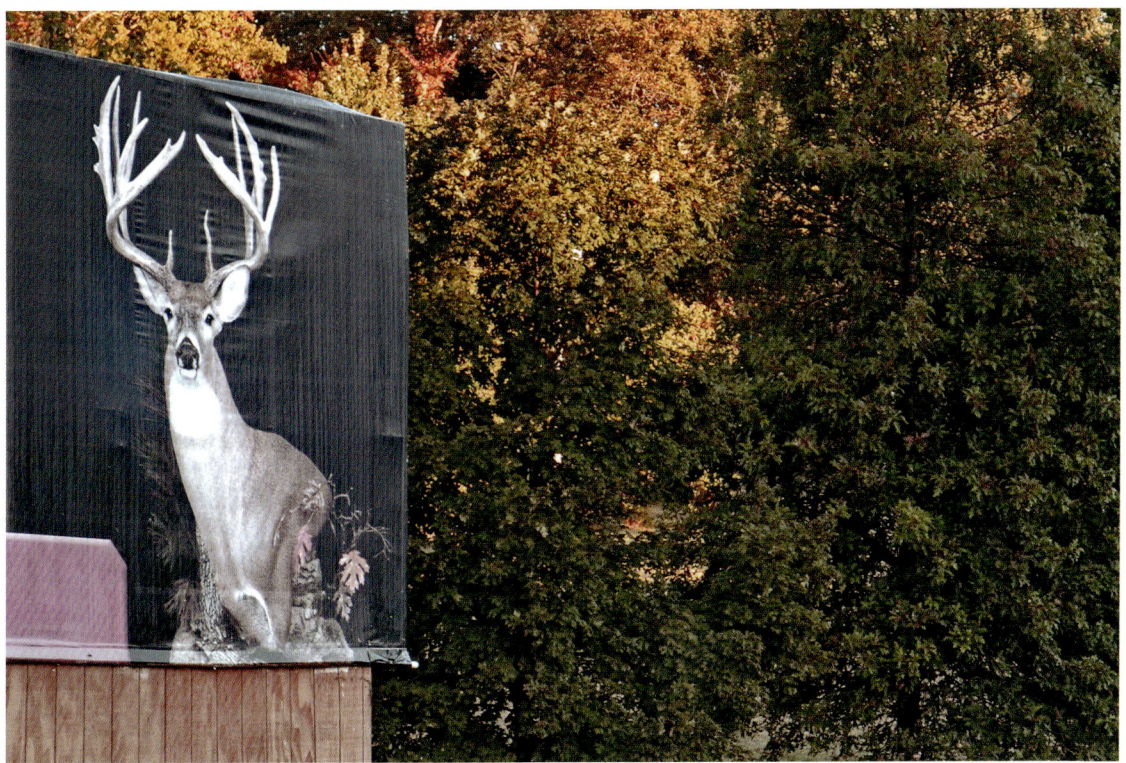

Malibu, California

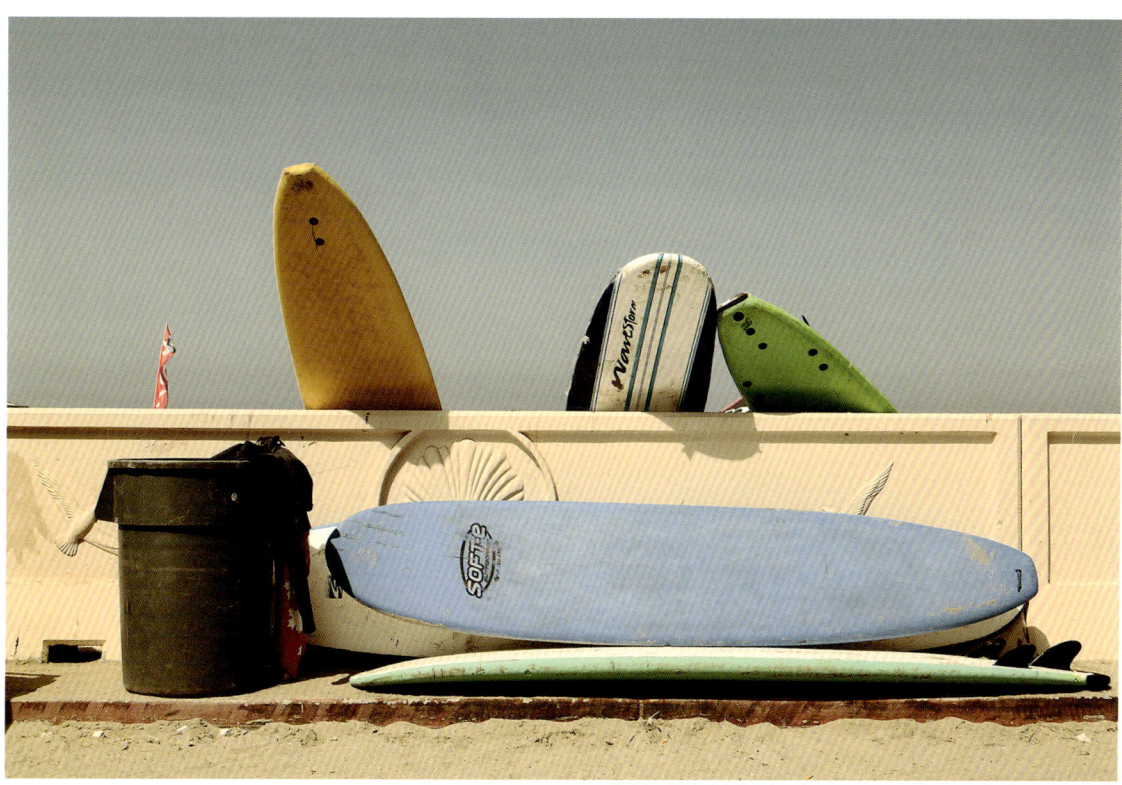

Lupton, Arizona

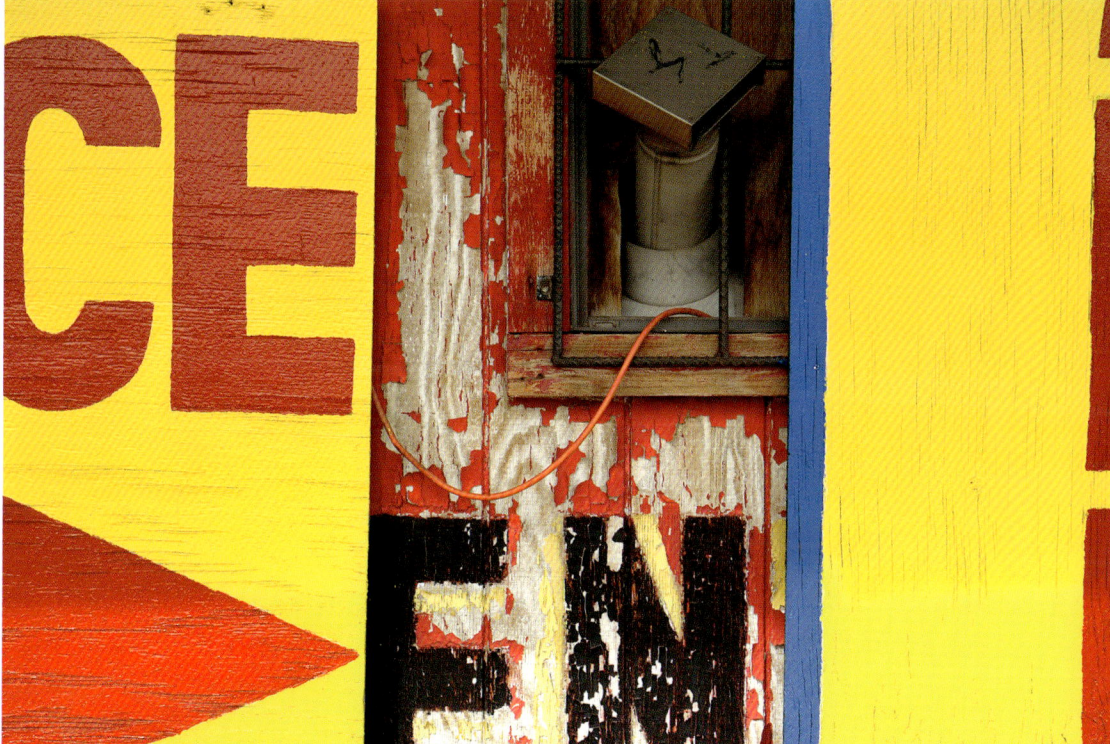

Kingman, Arizona

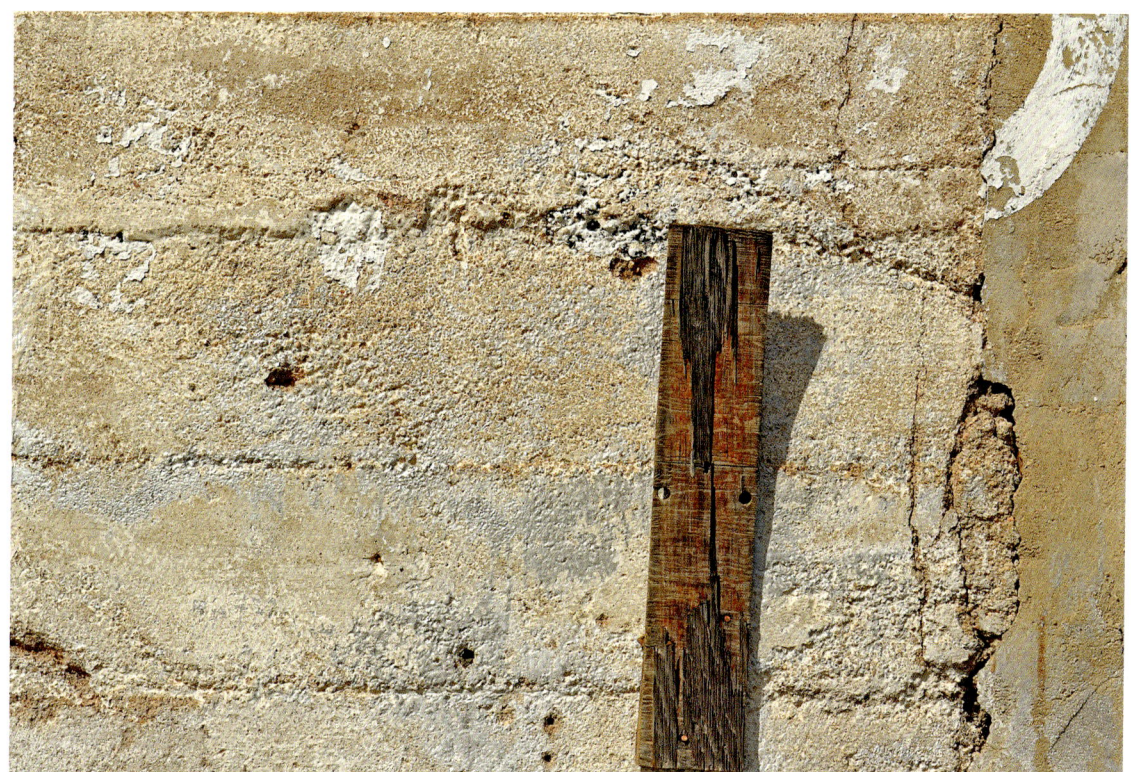

Penn Yan, New York

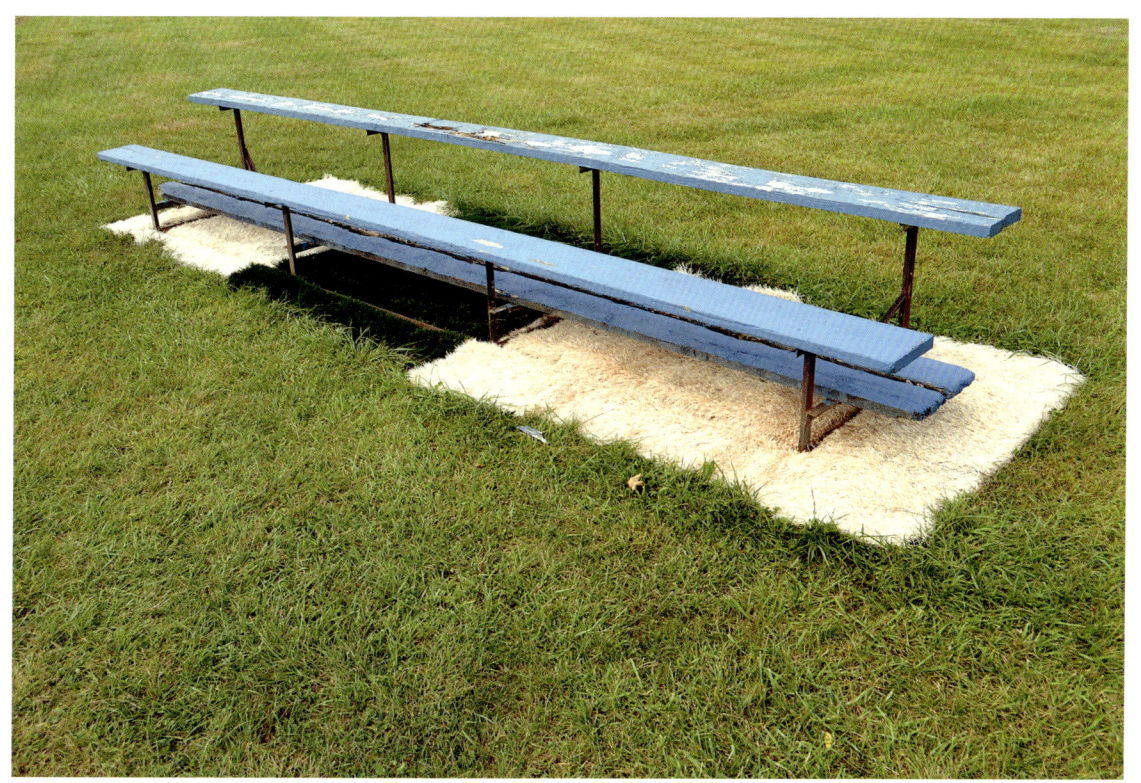

Abilene, Kansas

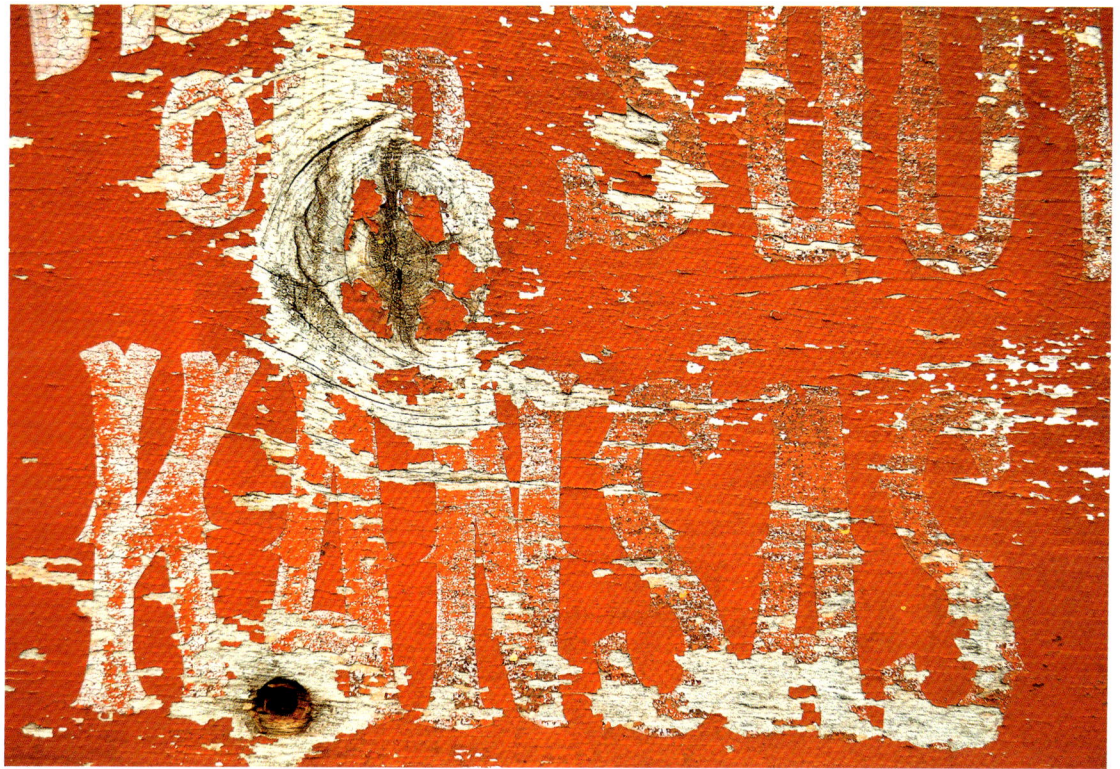

San Bernardino, California

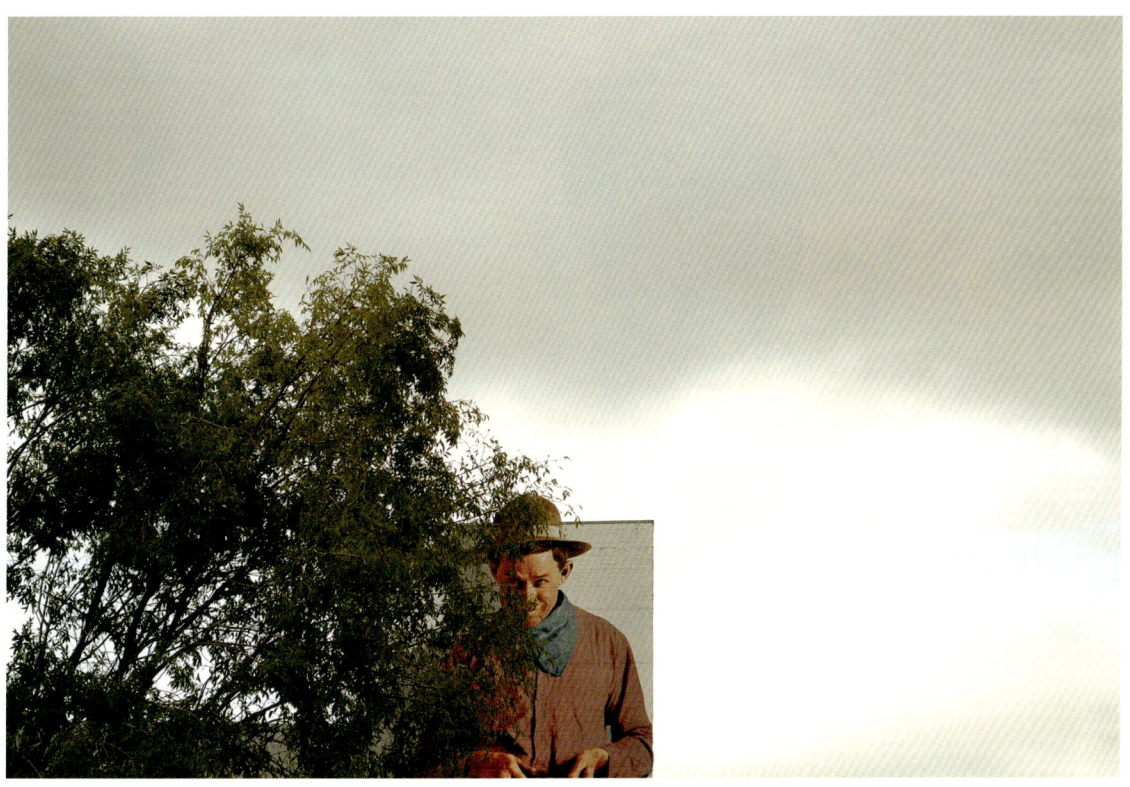

Kiowa, Colorado

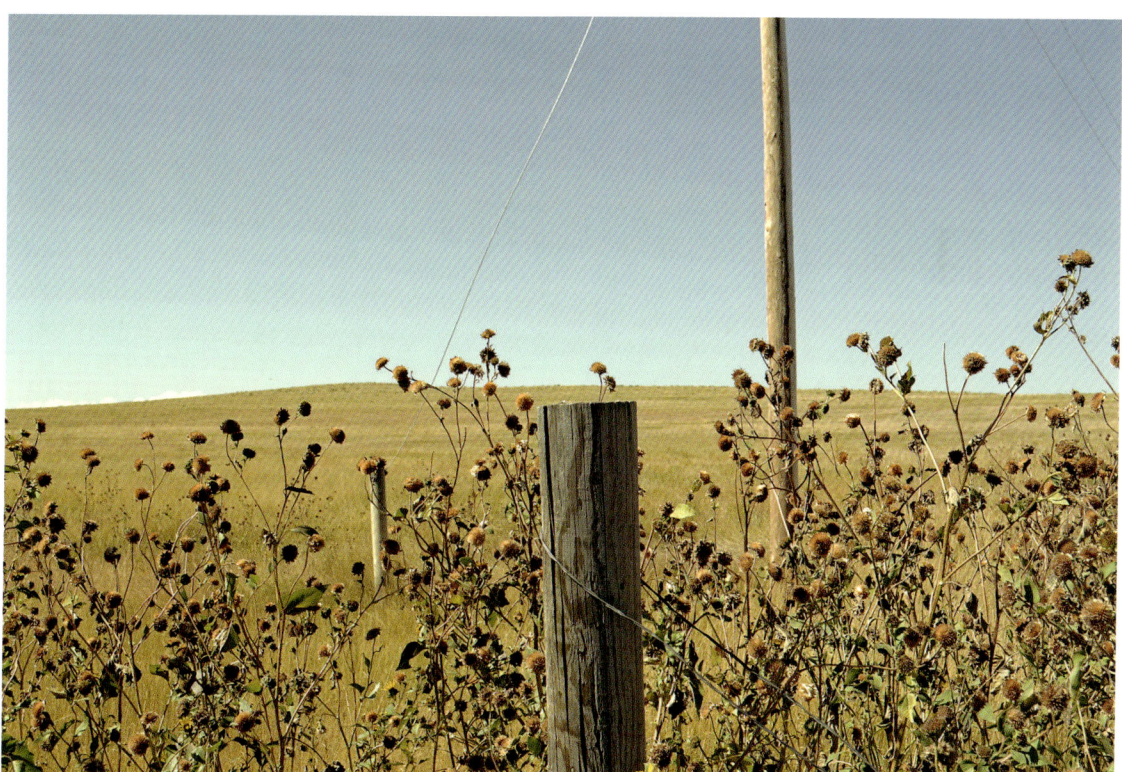

Scranton, Pennsylvania

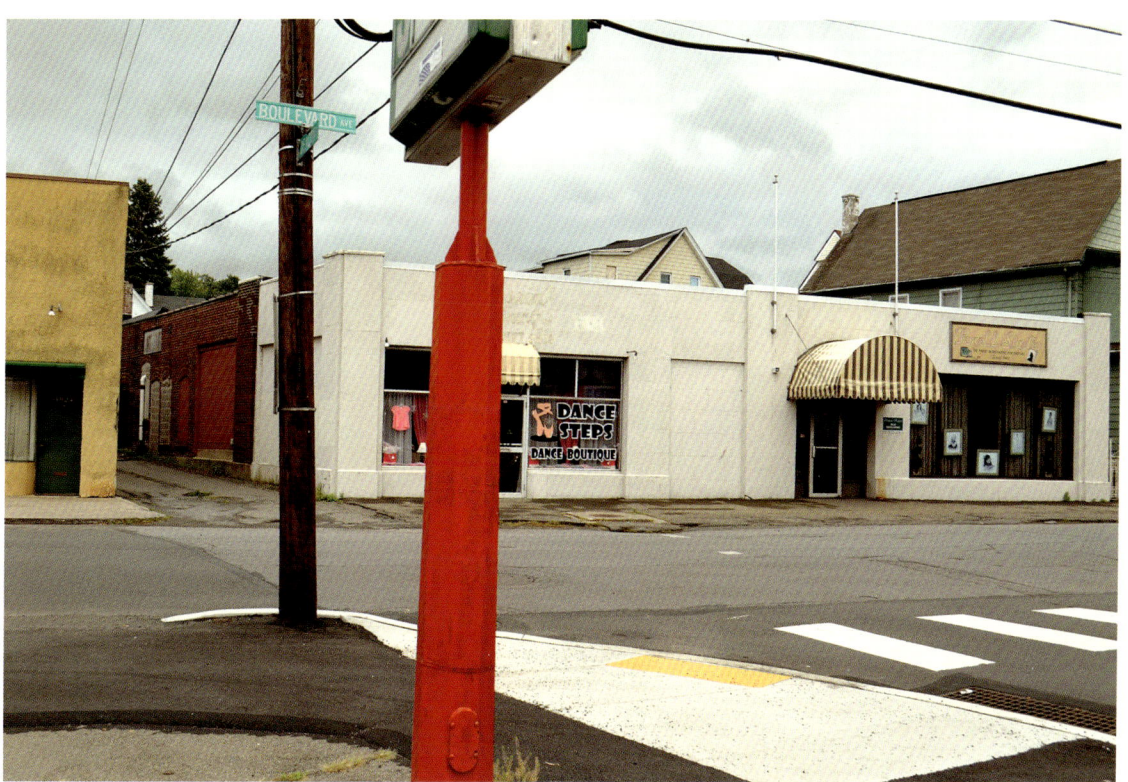

Coney Island, New York

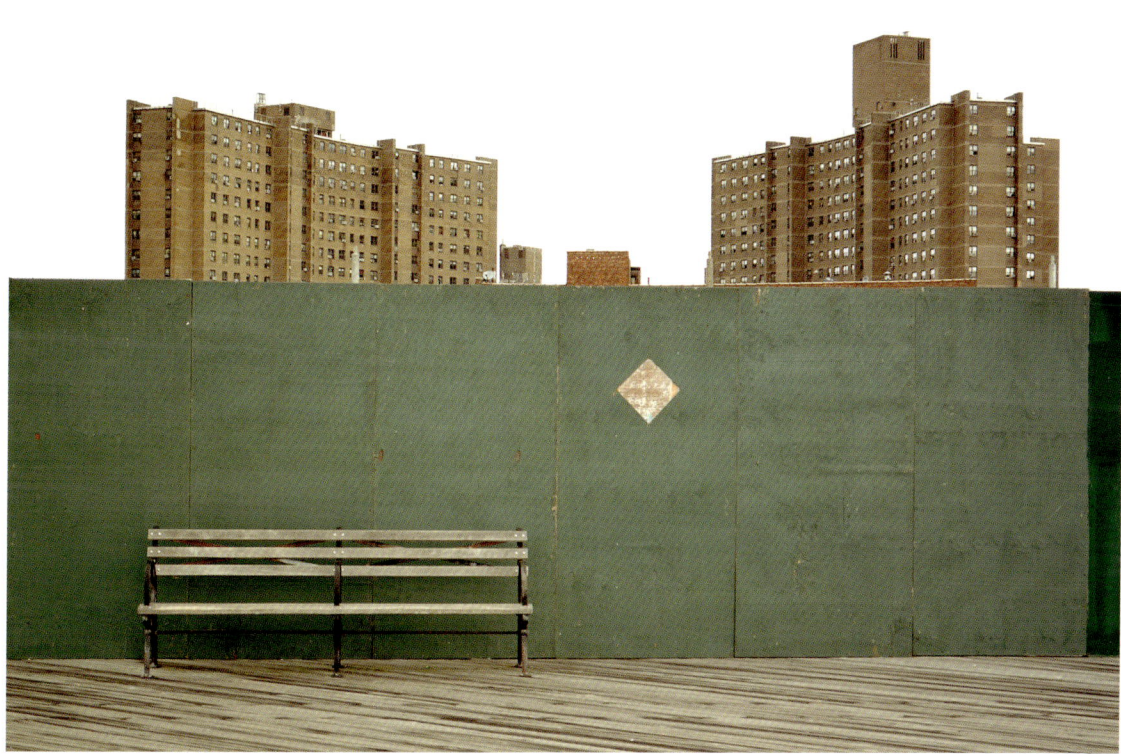

Taos County, New Mexico

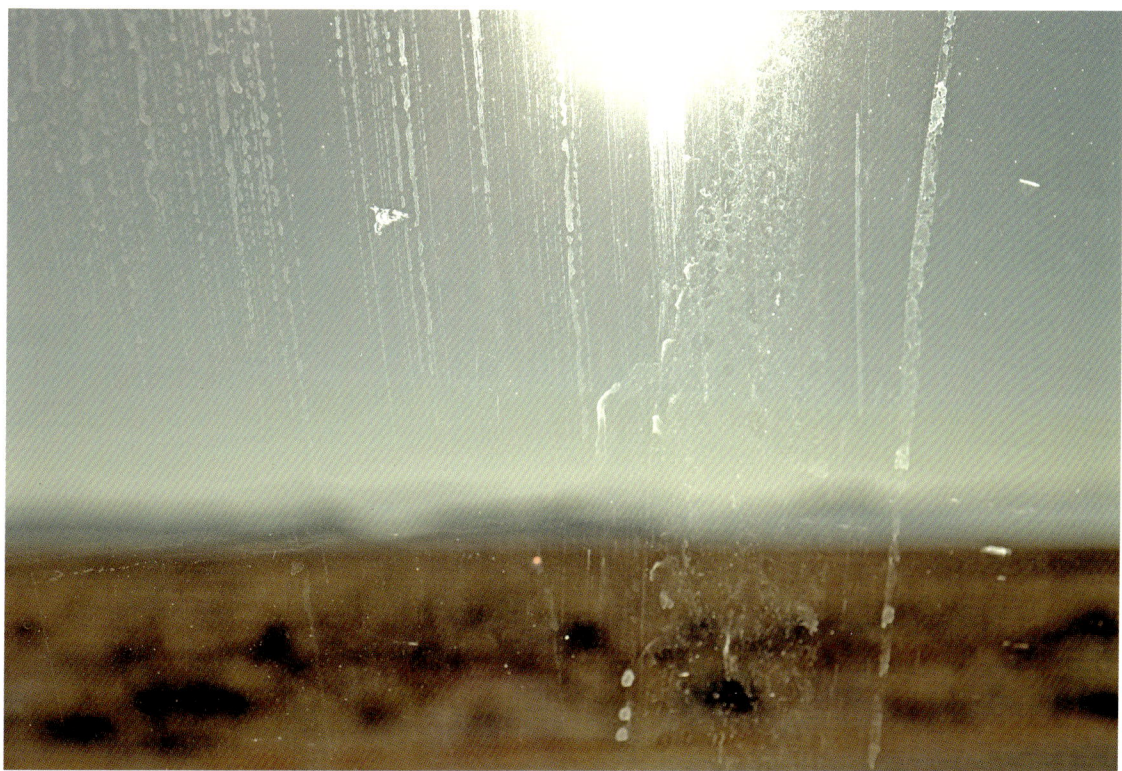

Cañon City, Colorado

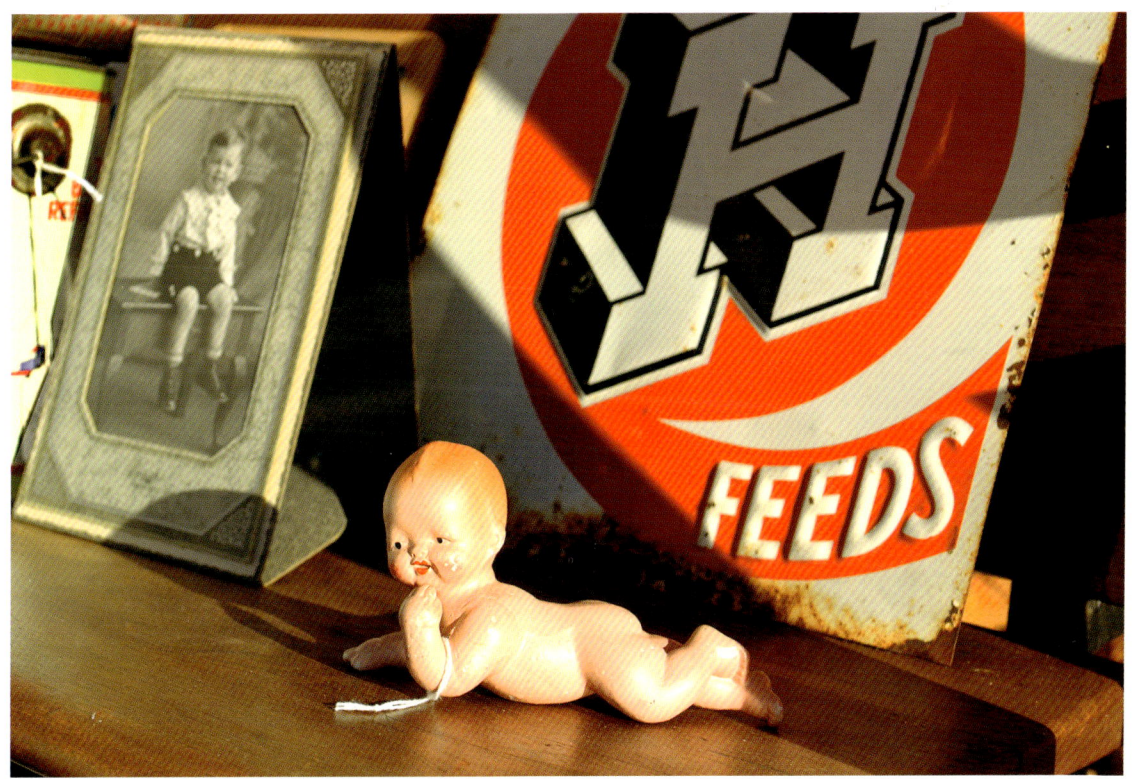

Primm, Nevada

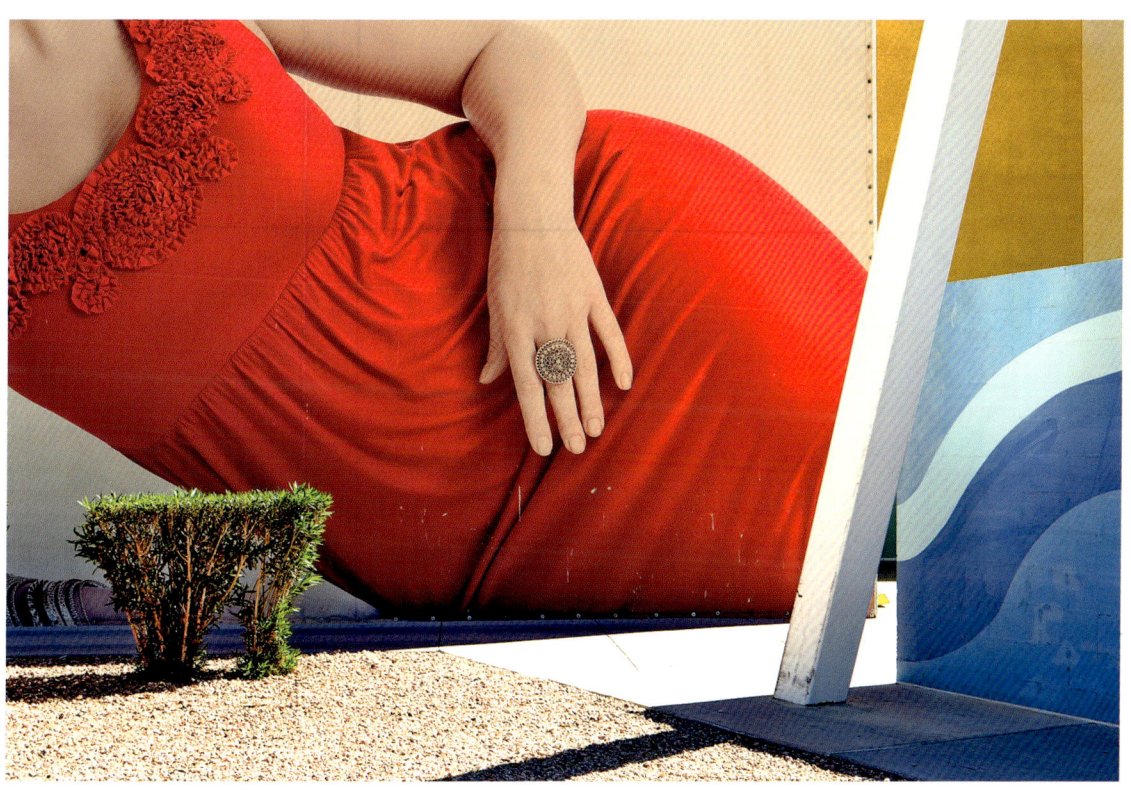

Colby, Kansas

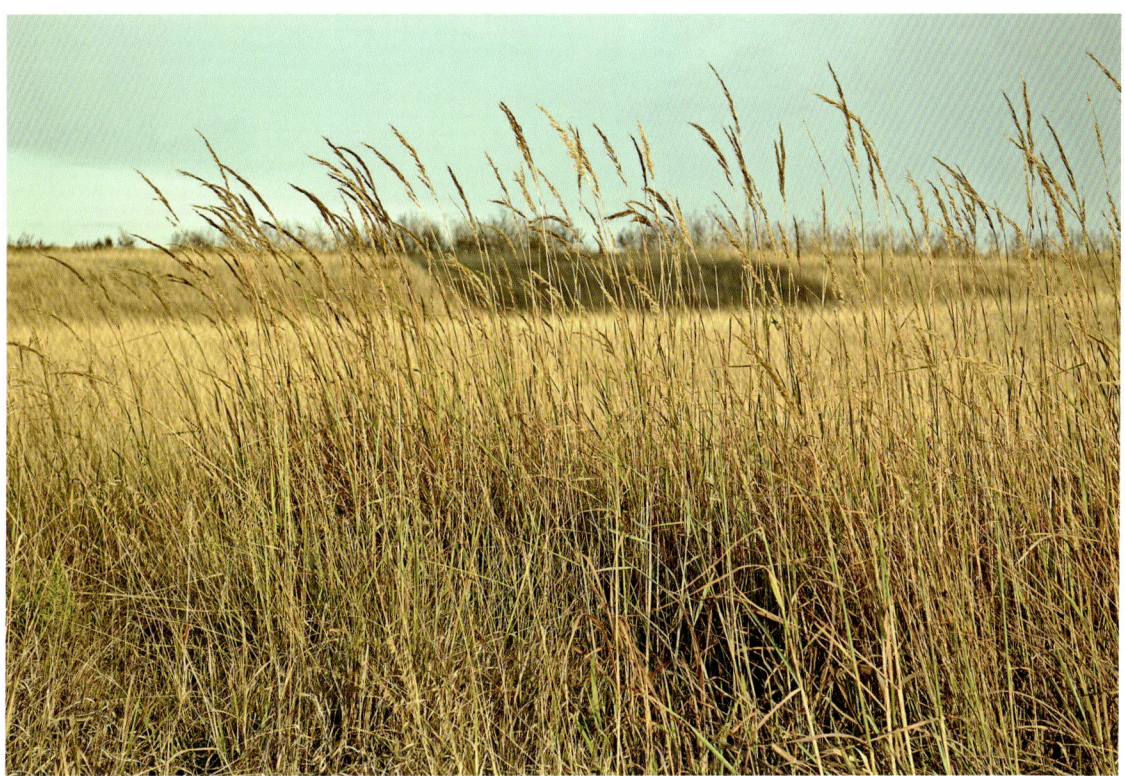

La Monte, Missouri

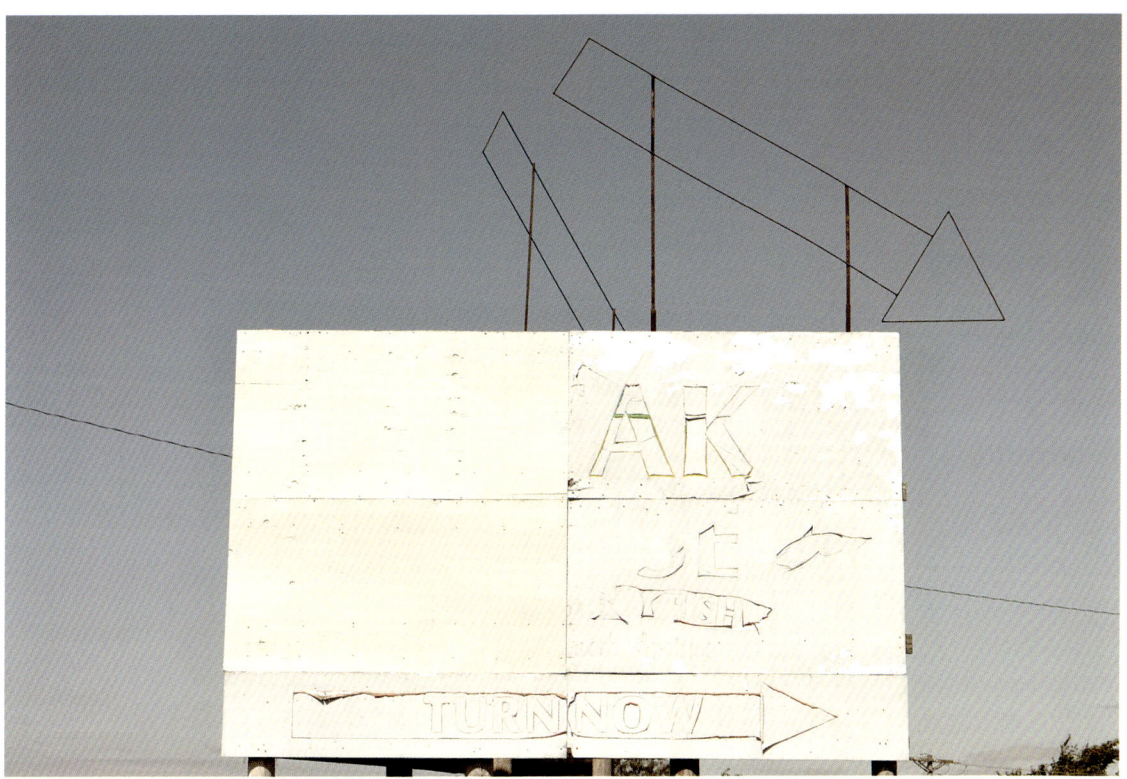

Rialto, California

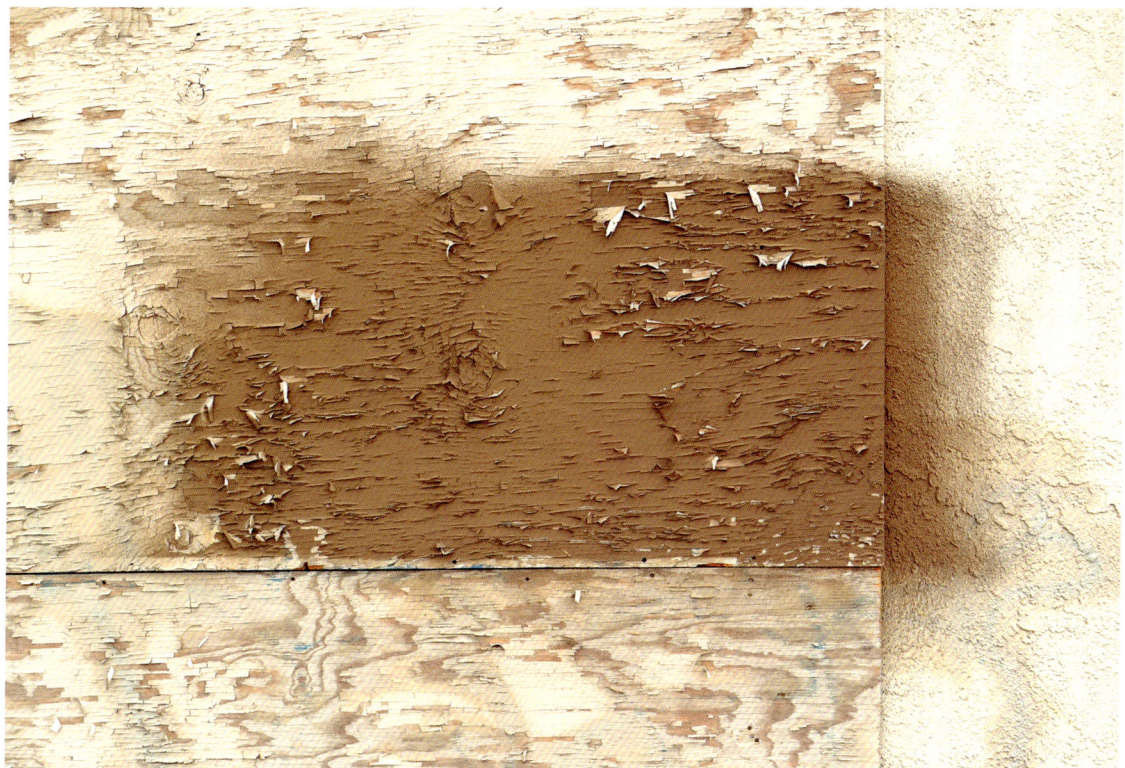

Seligman, Arizona

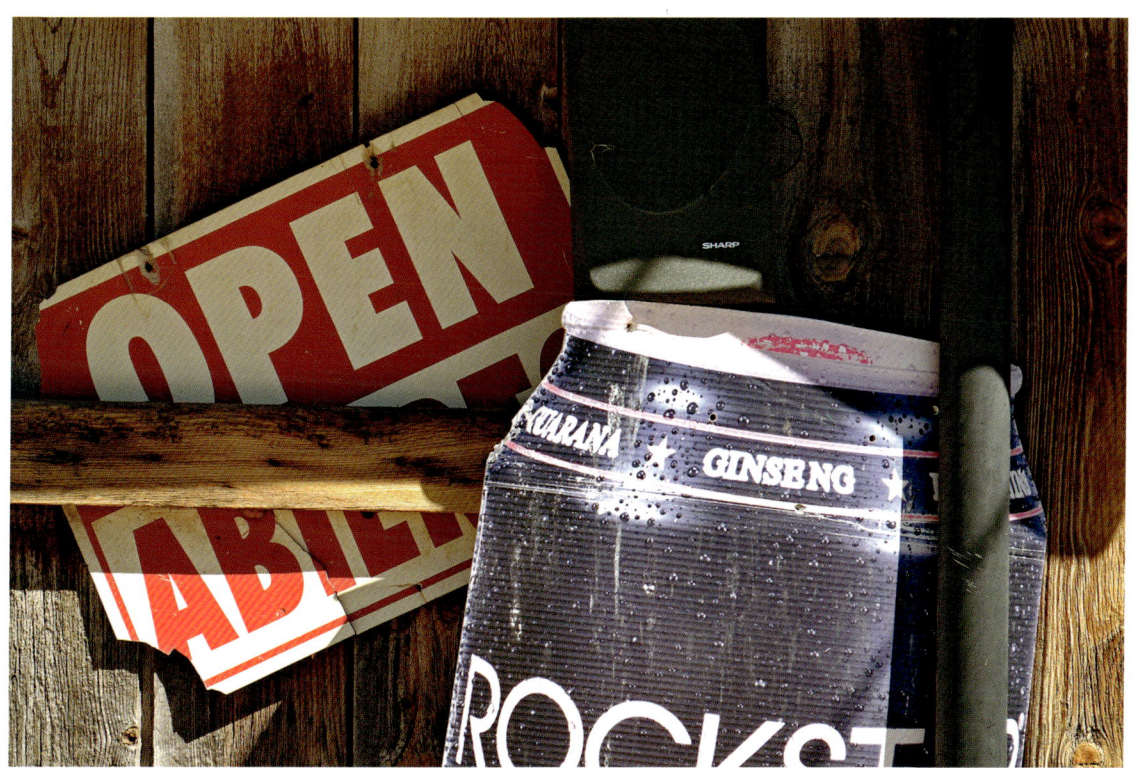

Shiprock, New Mexico

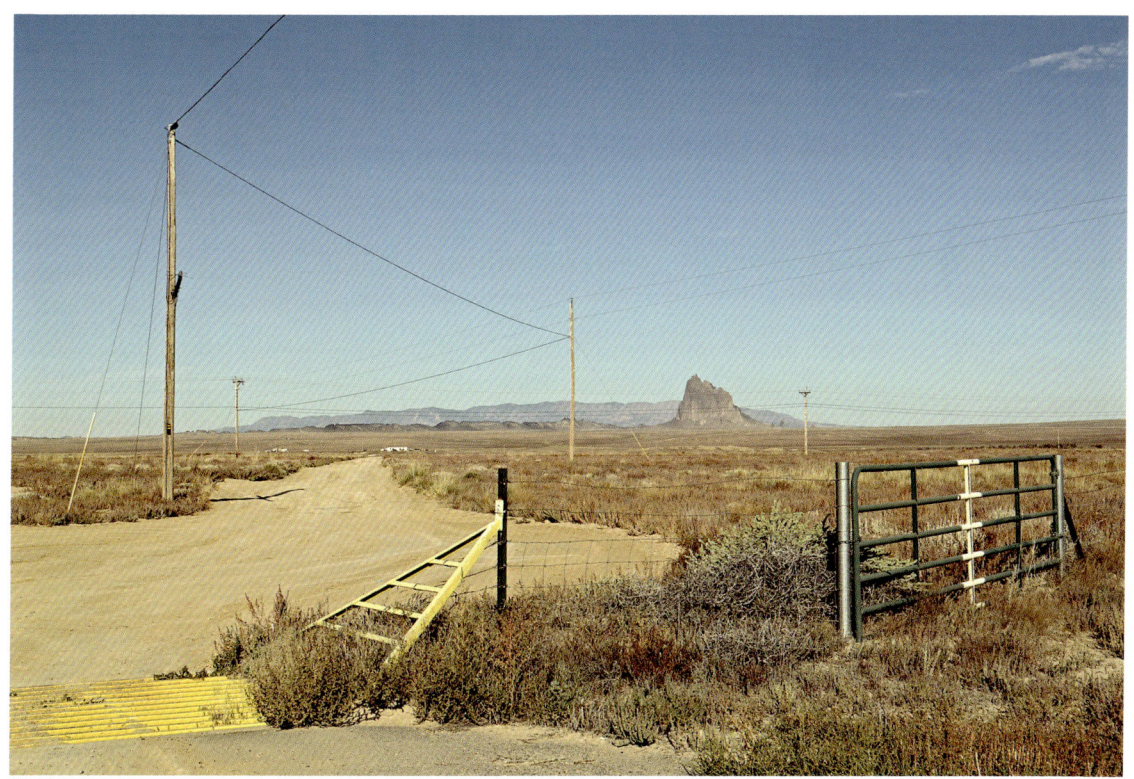

St. Joseph, Missouri

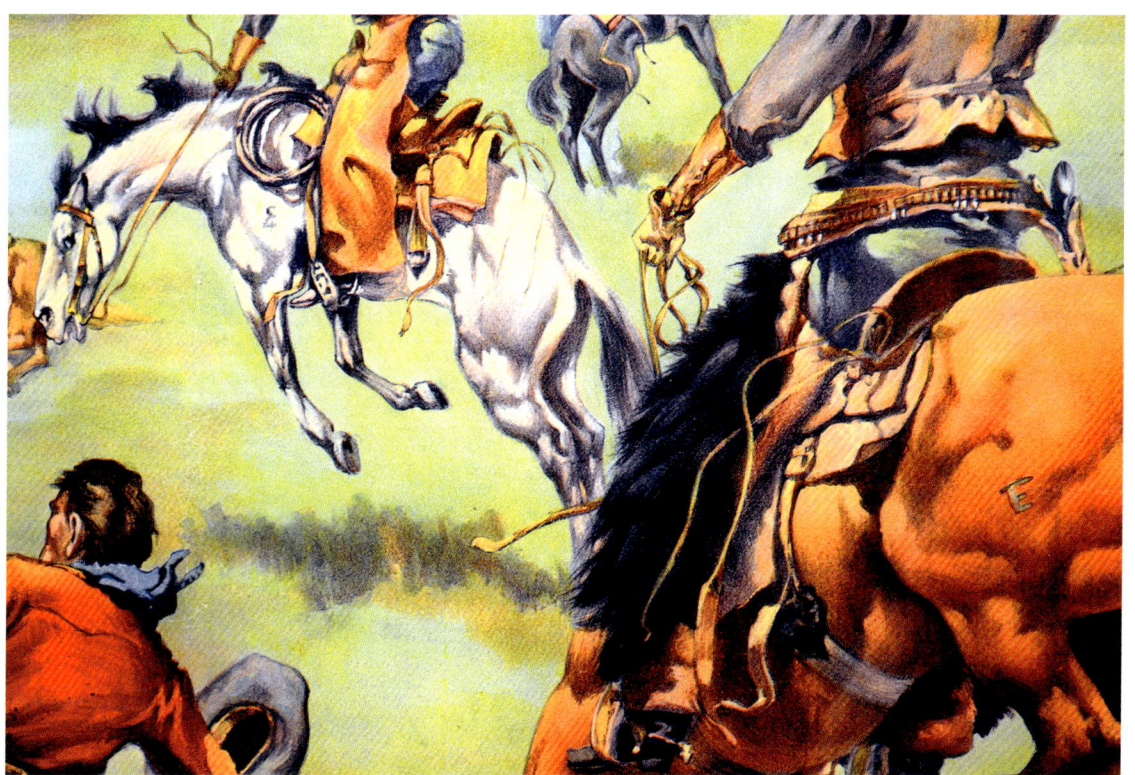

Winslow, Arizona

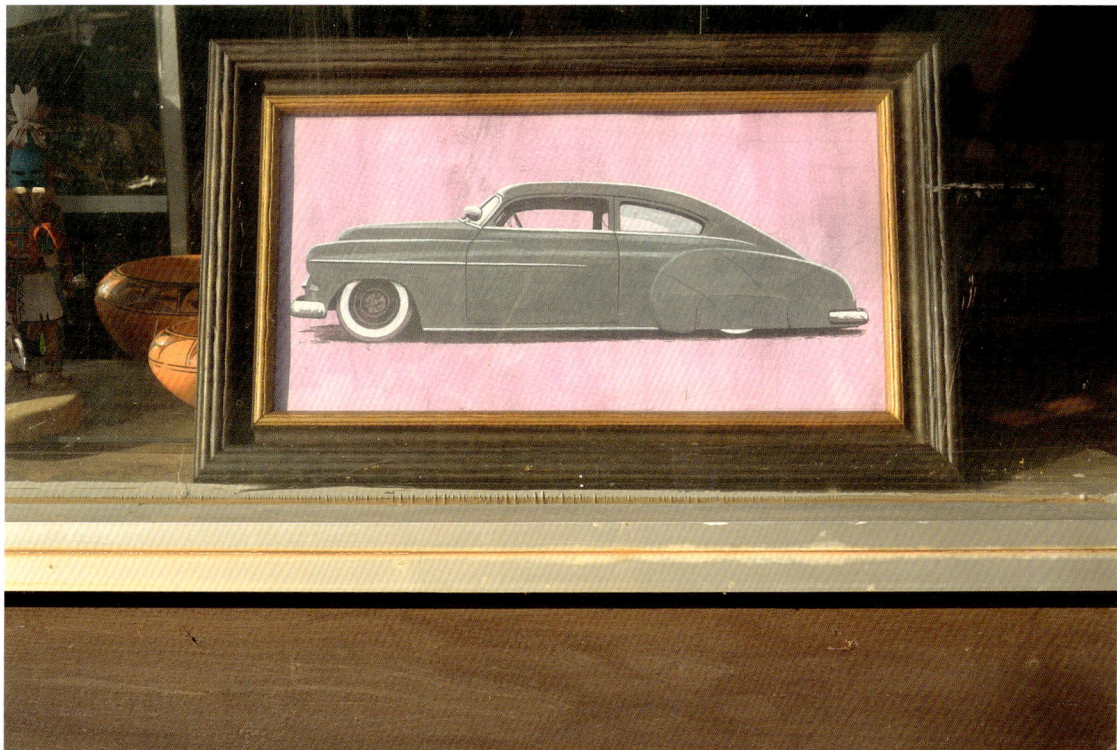

Scranton, Pennsylvania

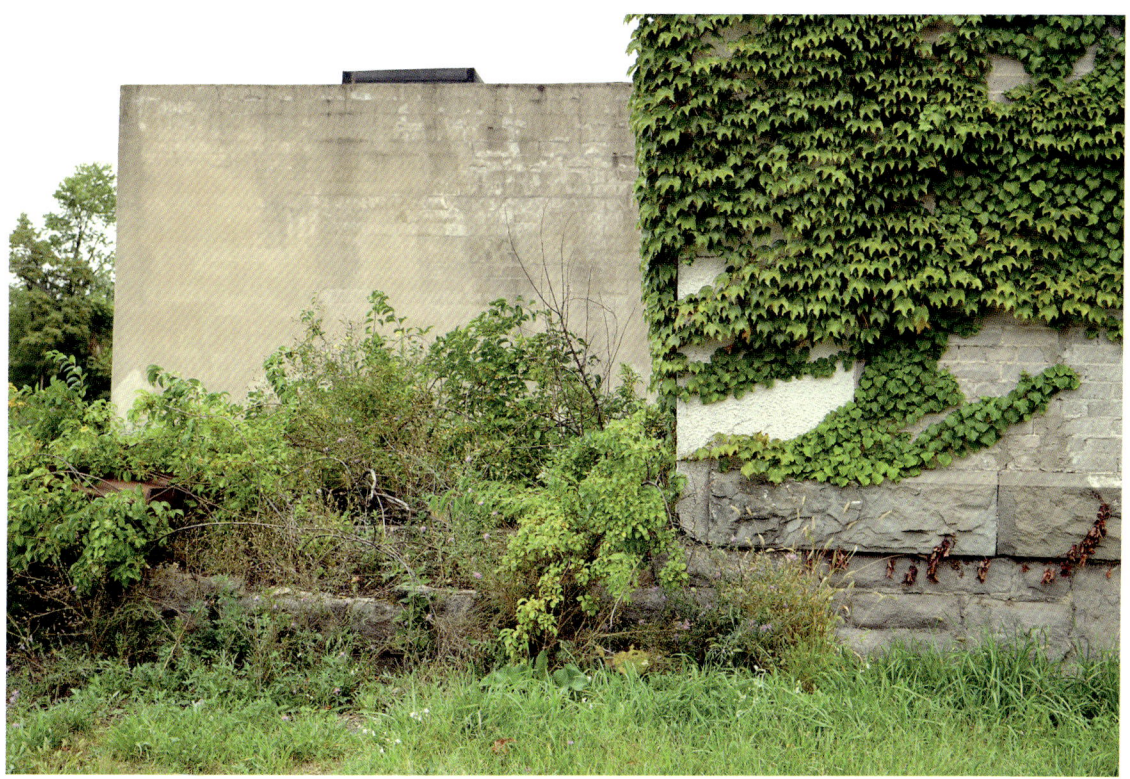

Stapleton, Colorado

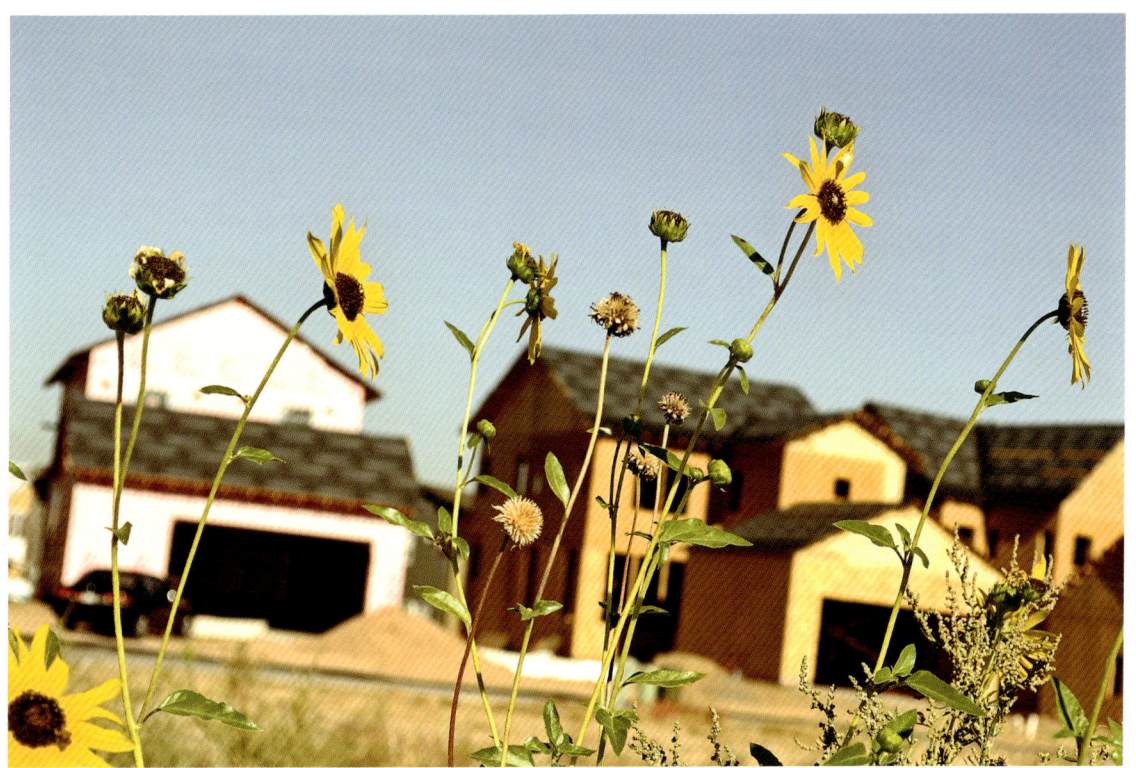

Kit Carson County, Colorado

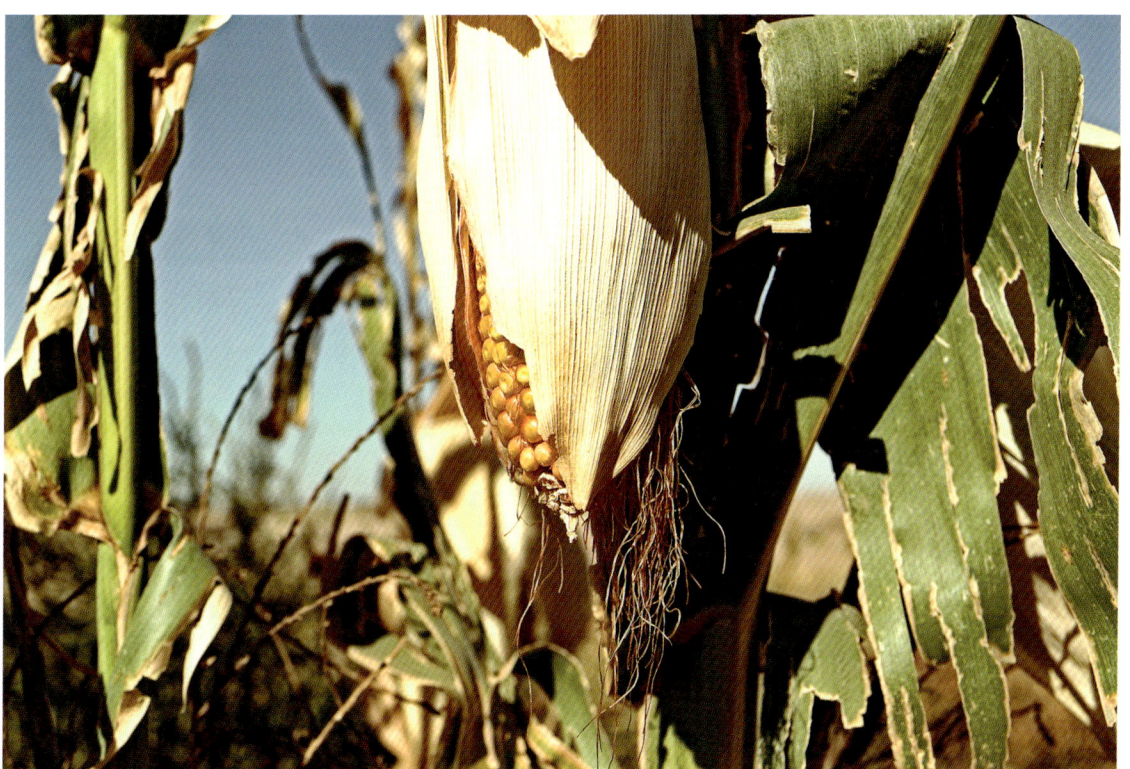

Bunker Hill, Kansas

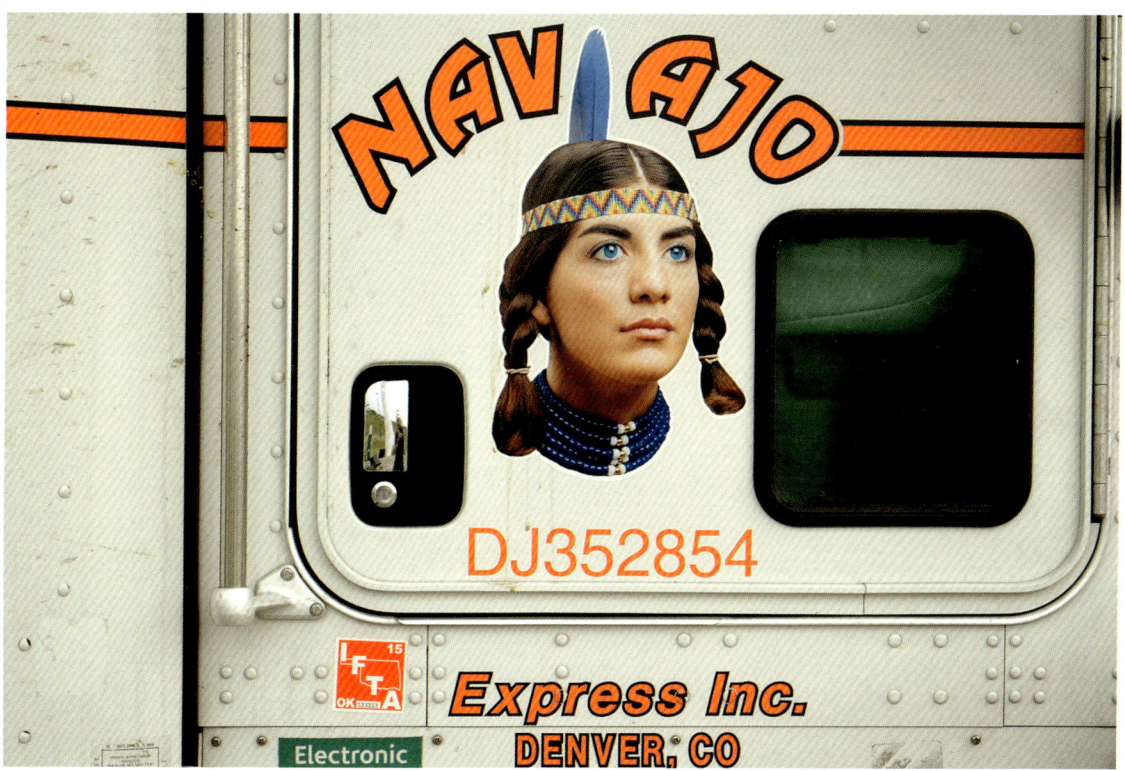

Chloride, Arizona

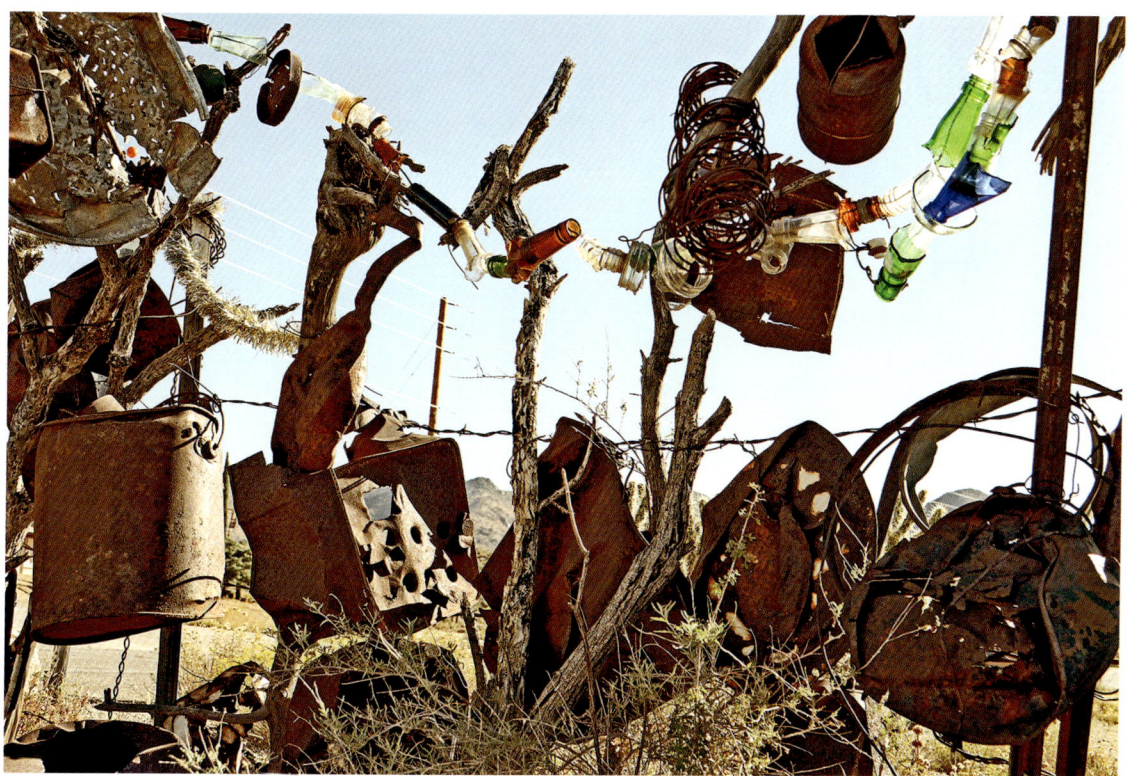

Abilene, Kansas

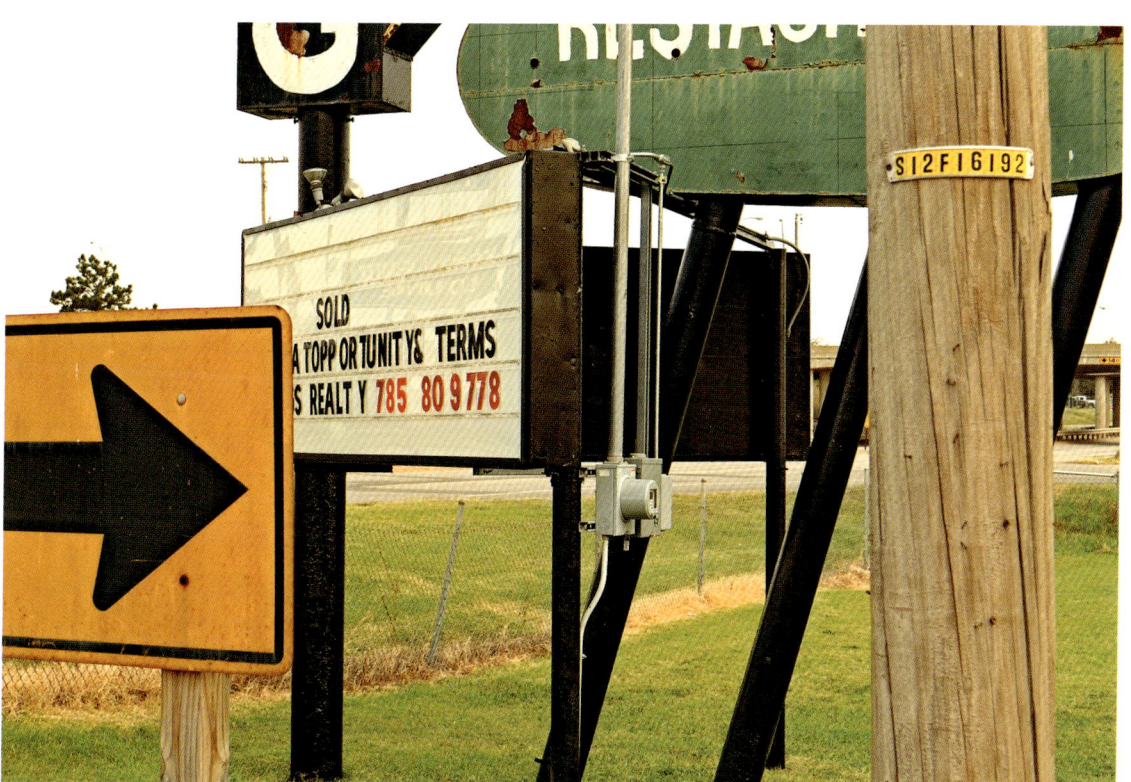

Holbrook, Arizona

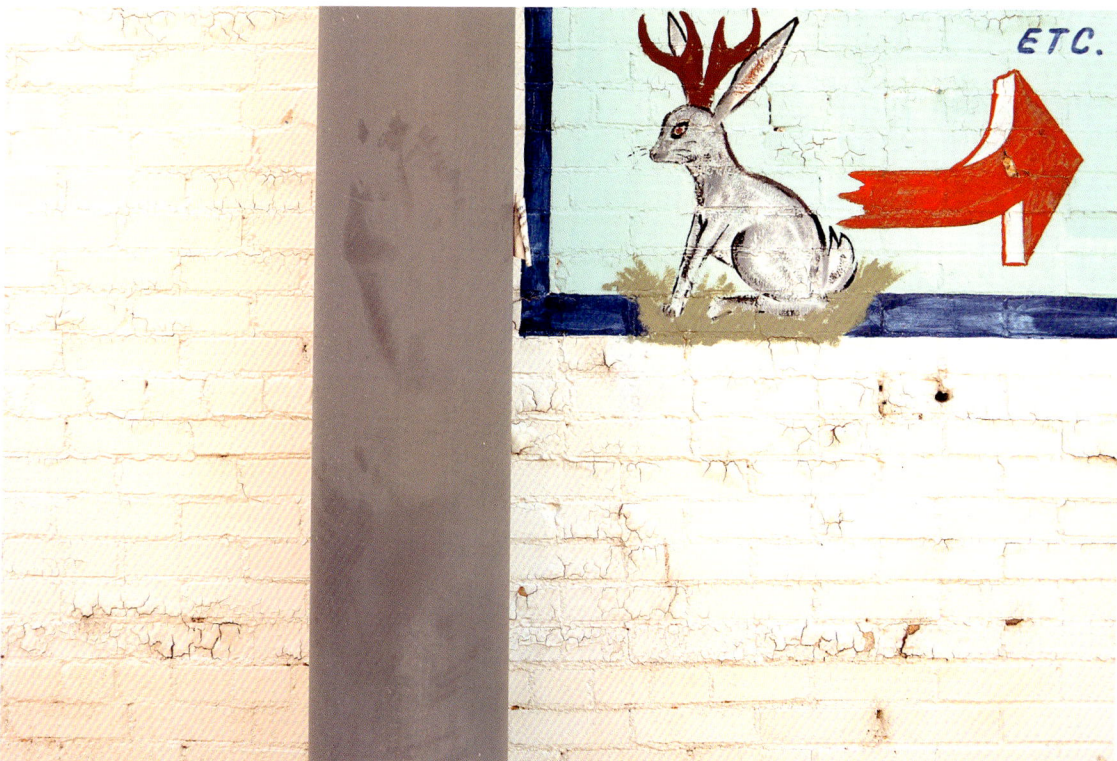

Higginsville, Missouri

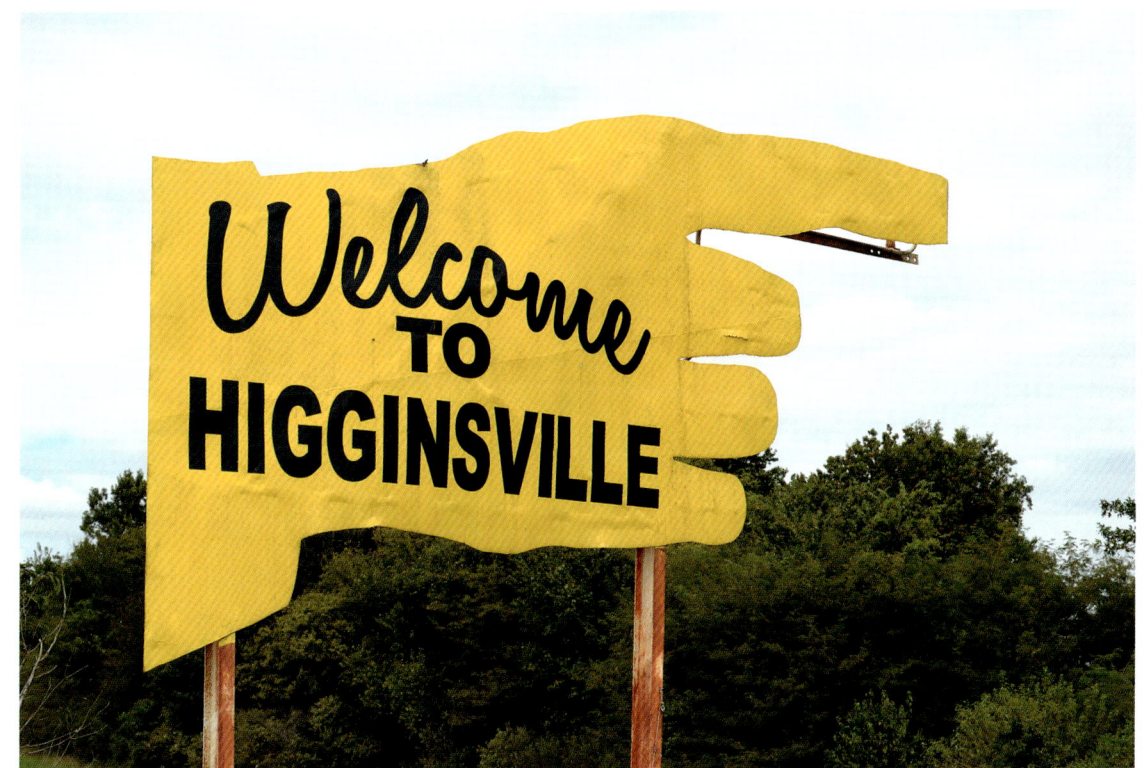

Cañon City, Colorado

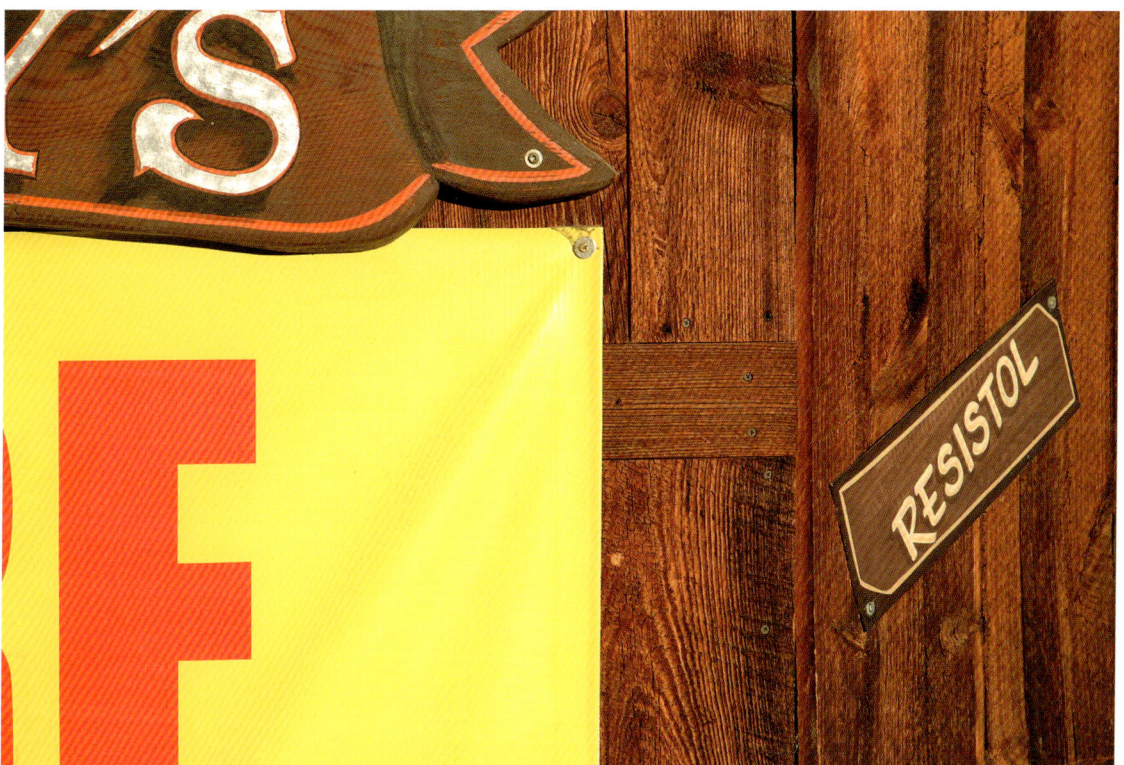

Pacific, Missouri

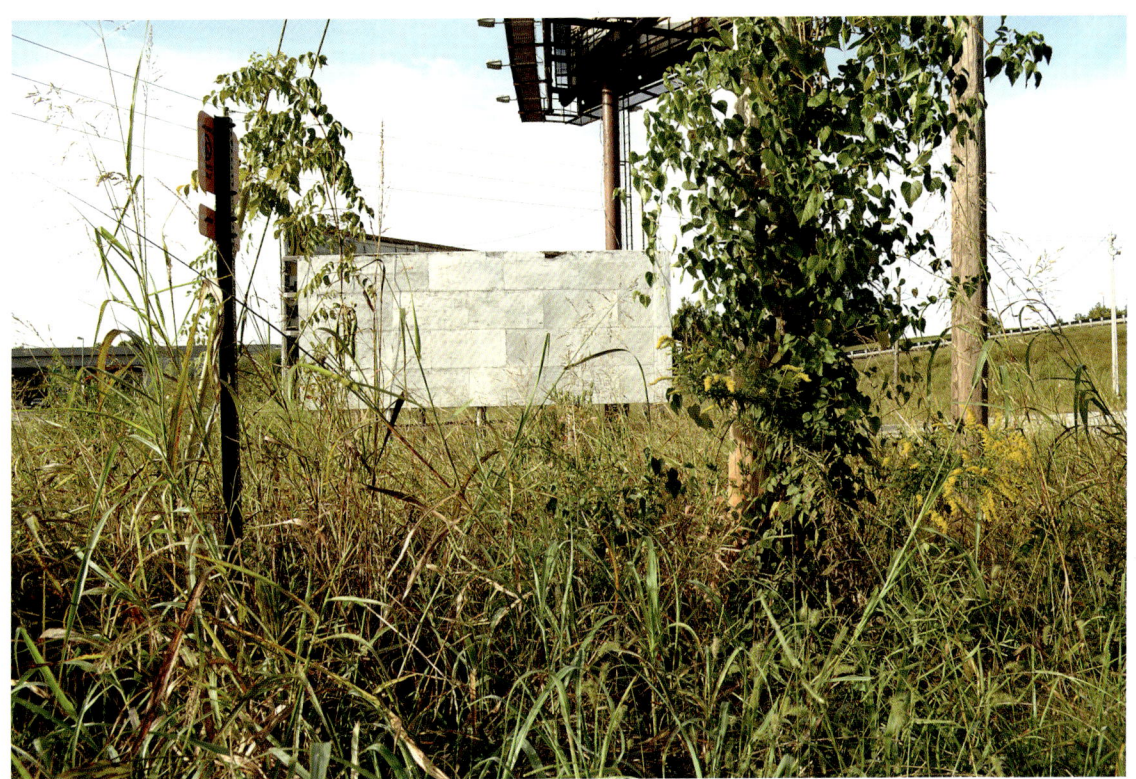

Toledo, Ohio

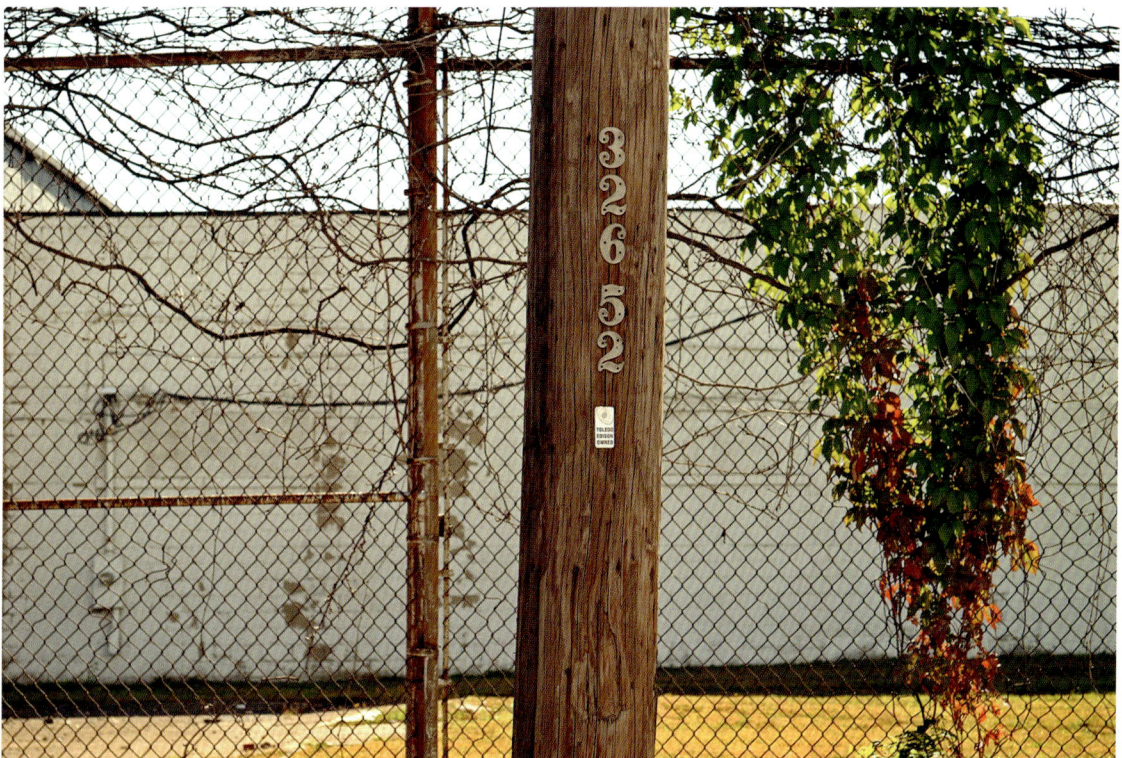

Kansas City, Missouri

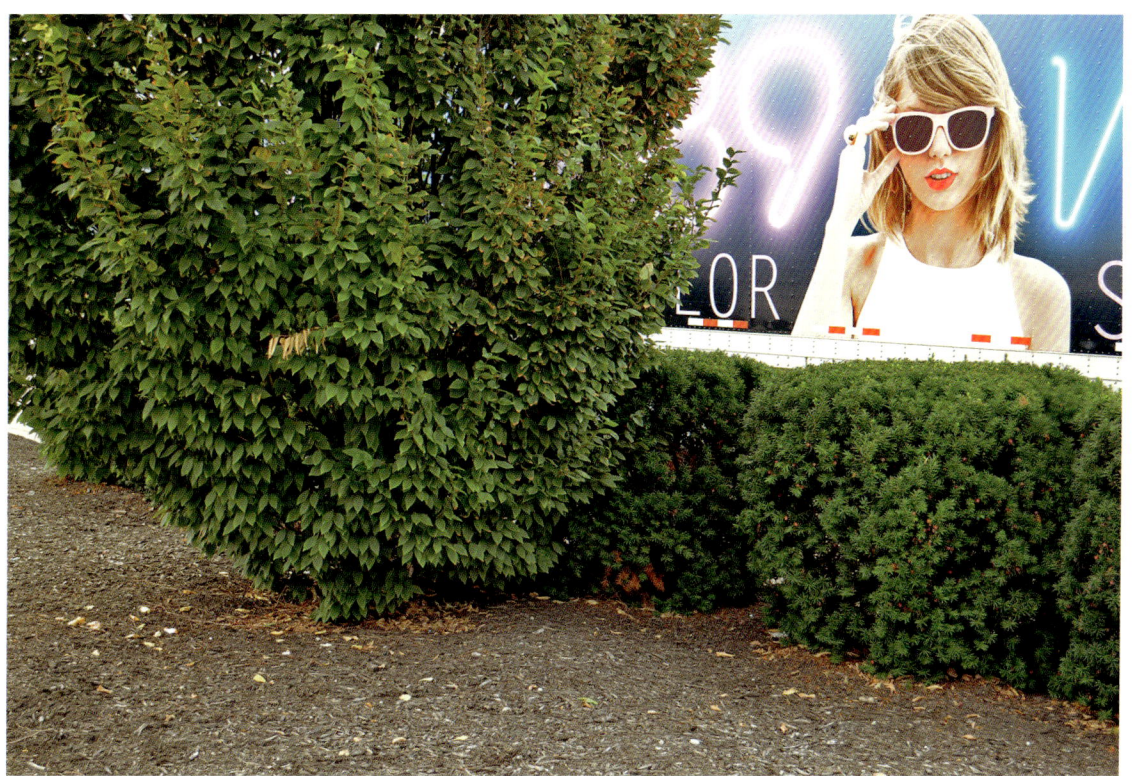

Boulder City, Nevada

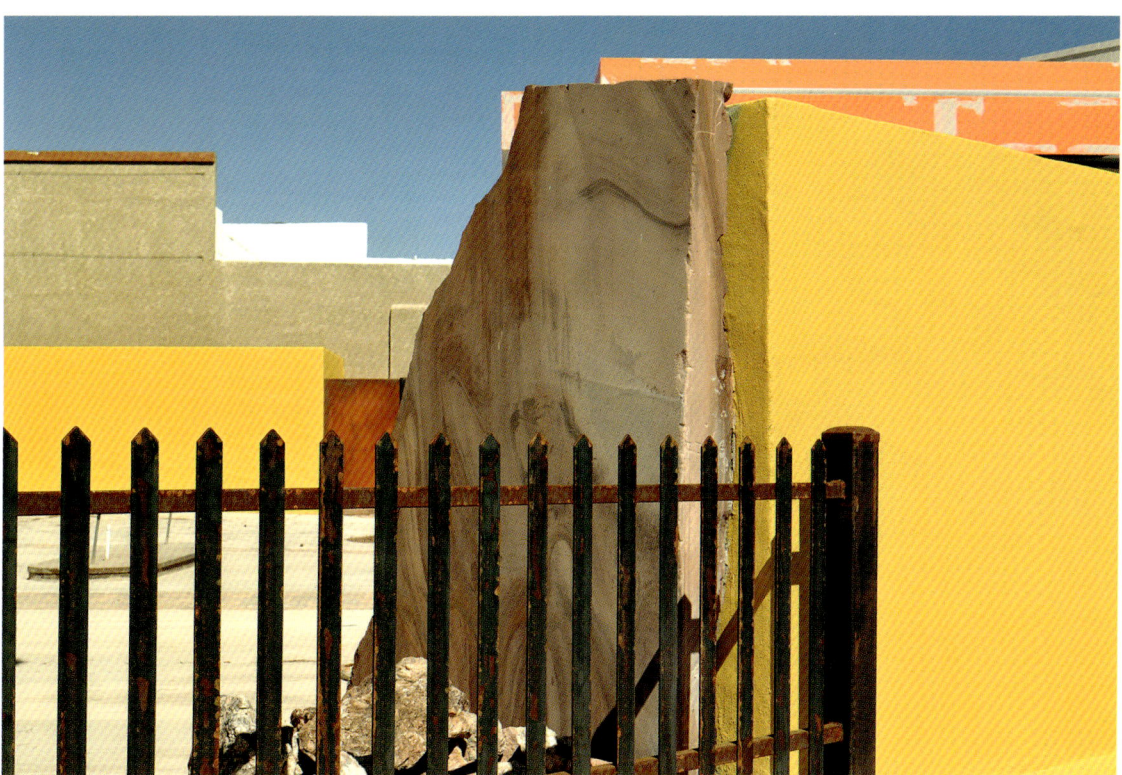

Bourbon, Missouri

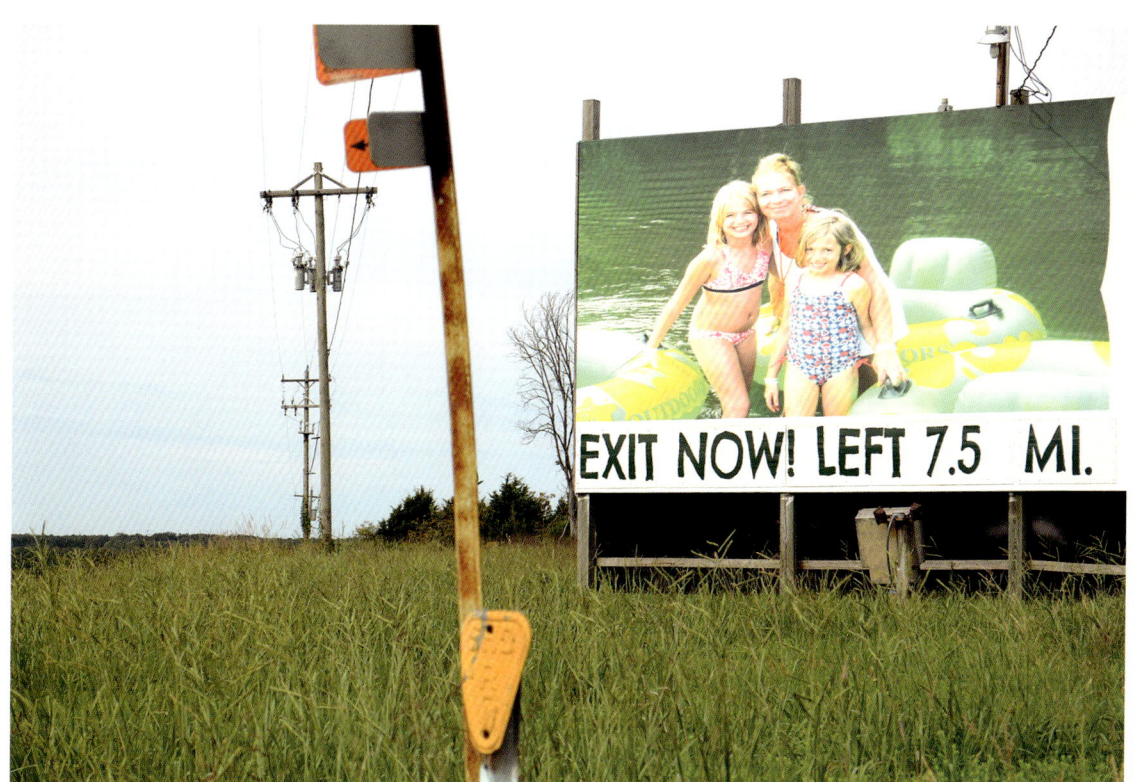

Royal Gorge, Colorado

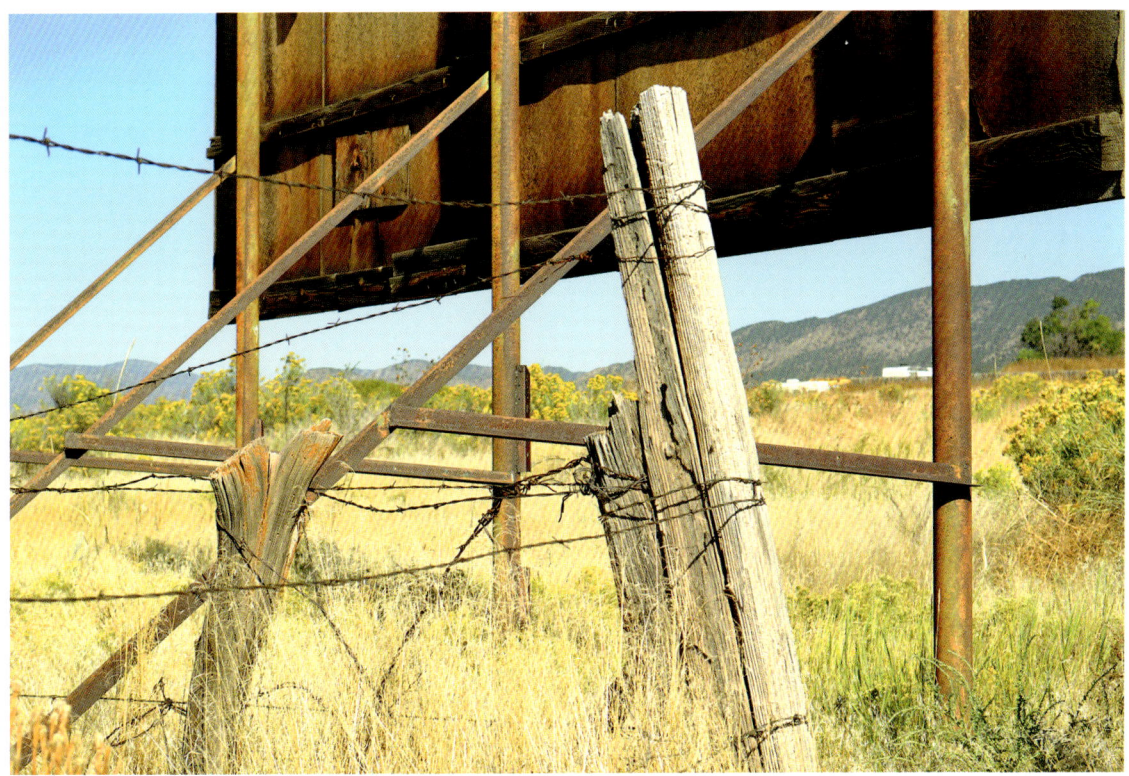

Chloride, Arizona

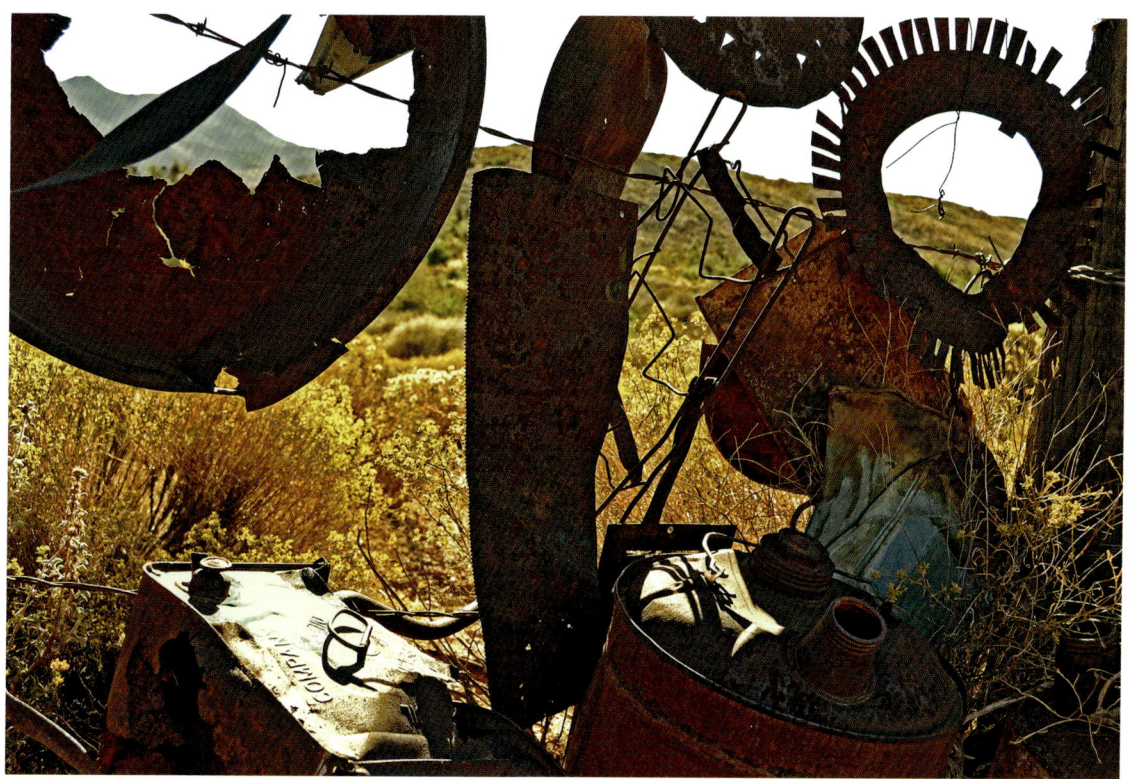

Junction City, Kansas

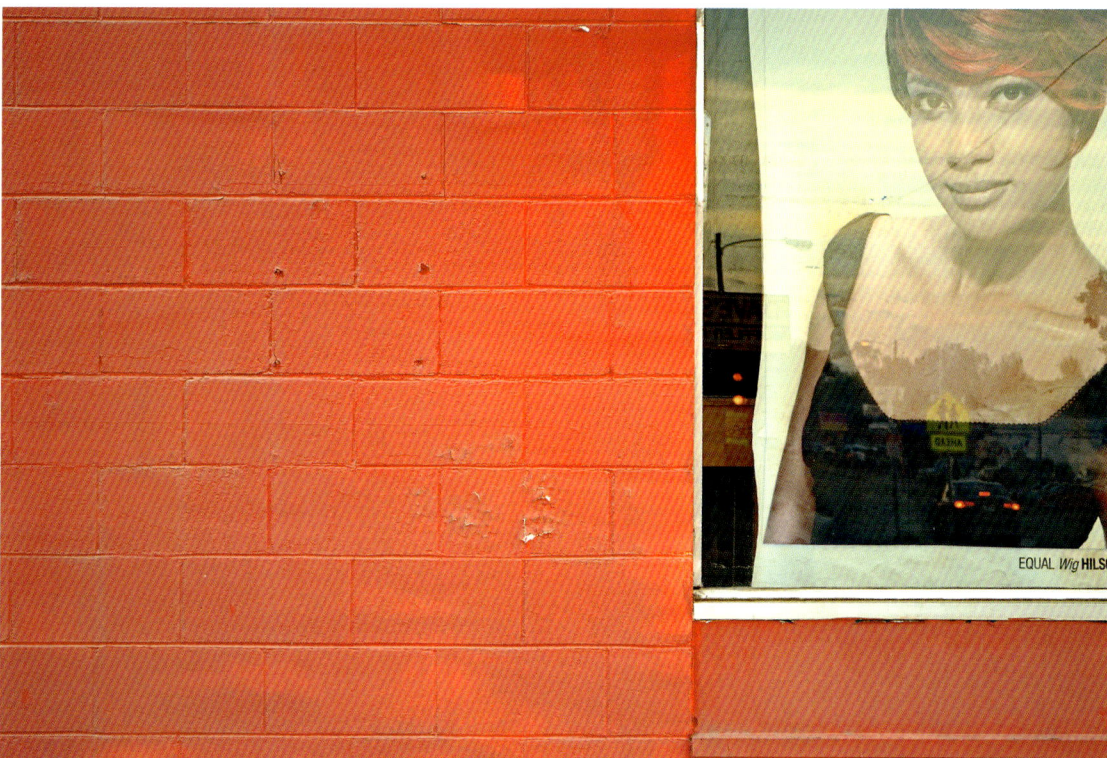

Kingman, Arizona

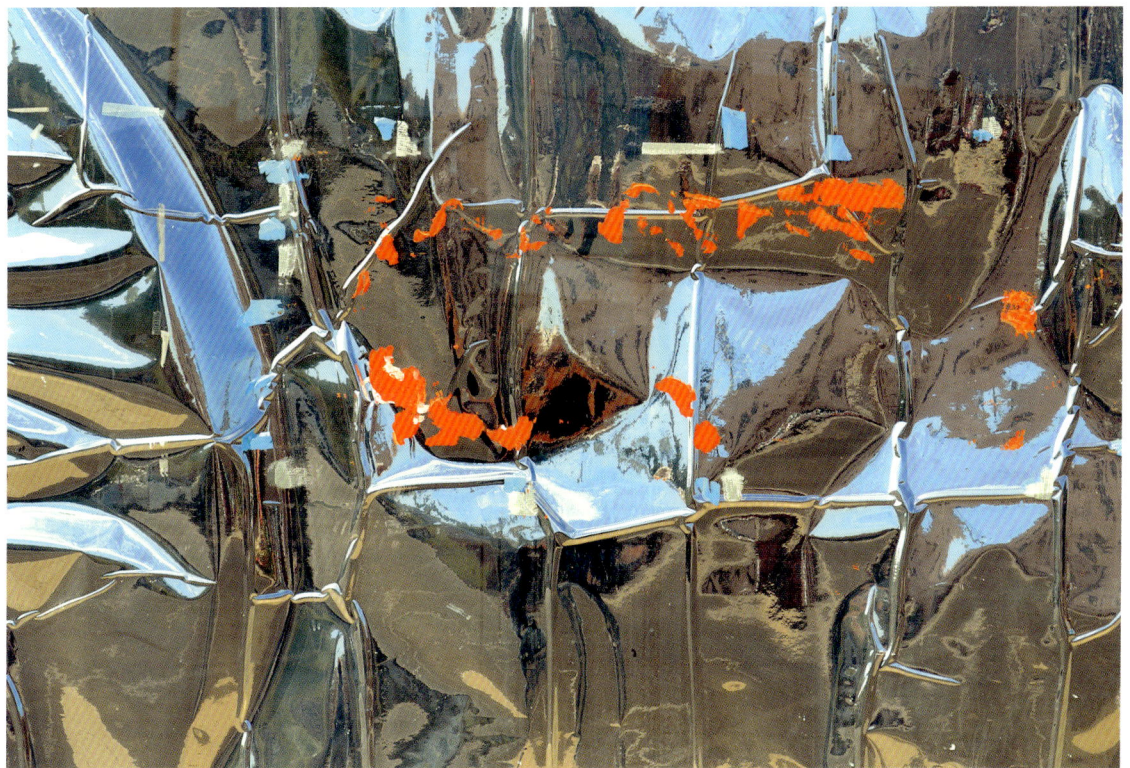

Las Vegas, Nevada

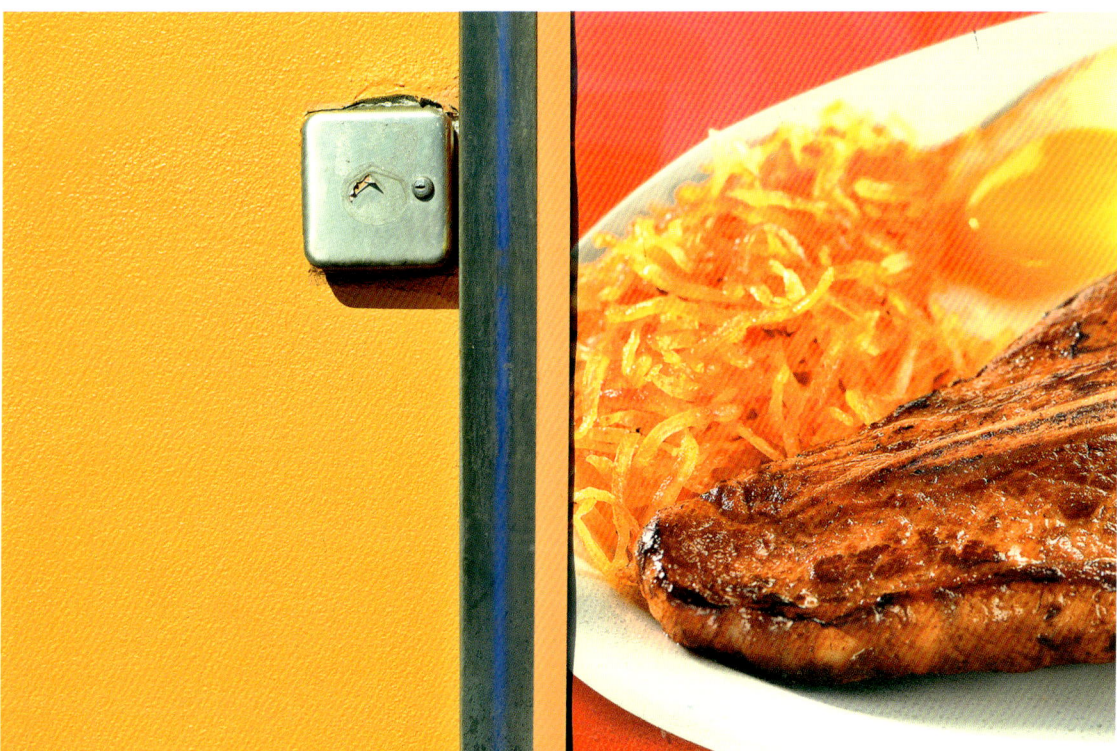

Boulder City, Nevada

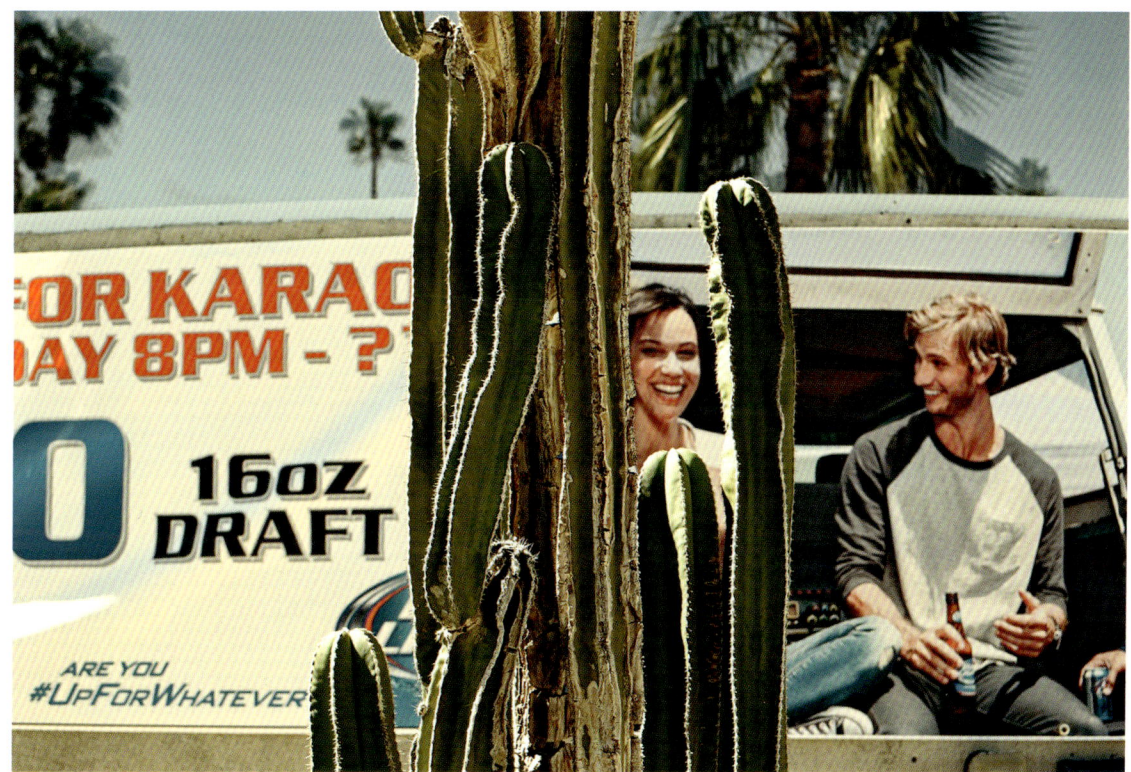

Sherman Oaks, California

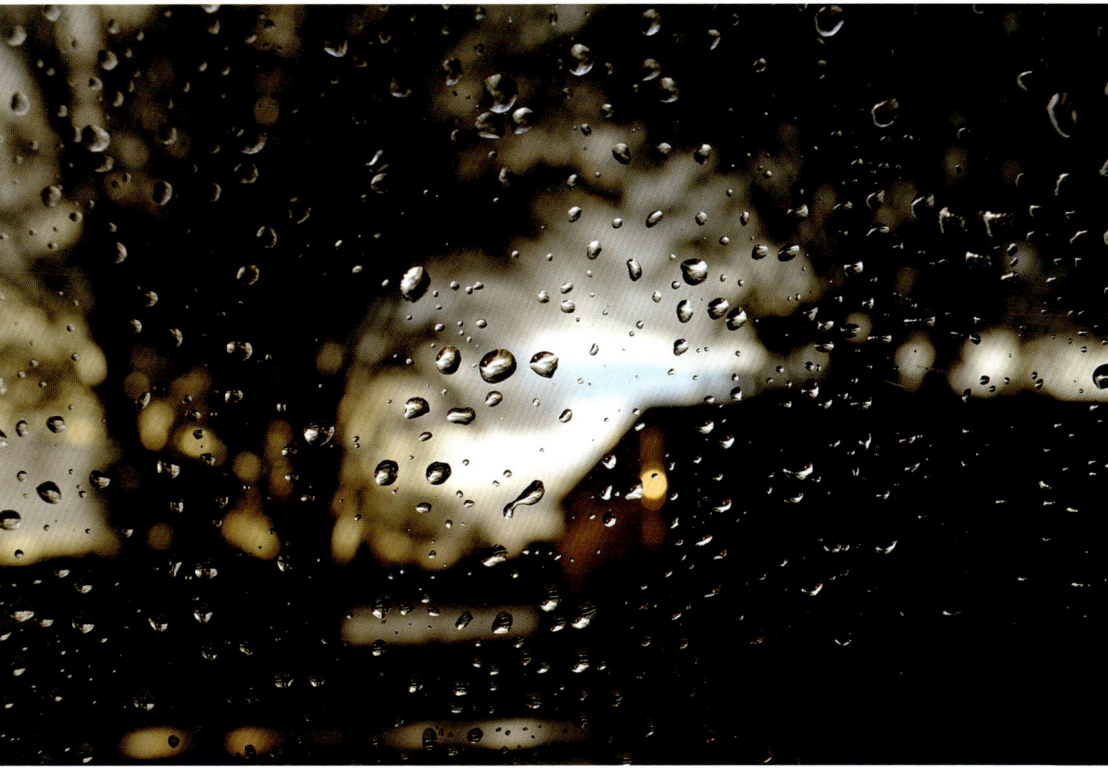

Yavapai County, Arizona

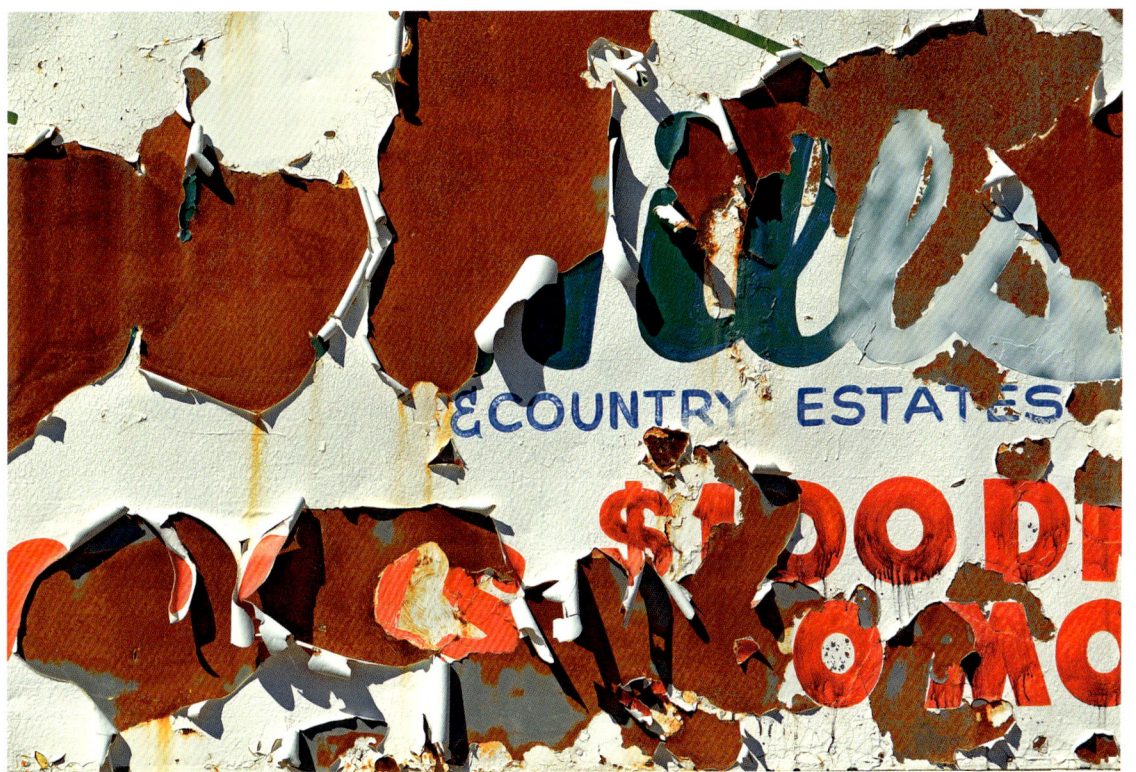

Coney Island, New York

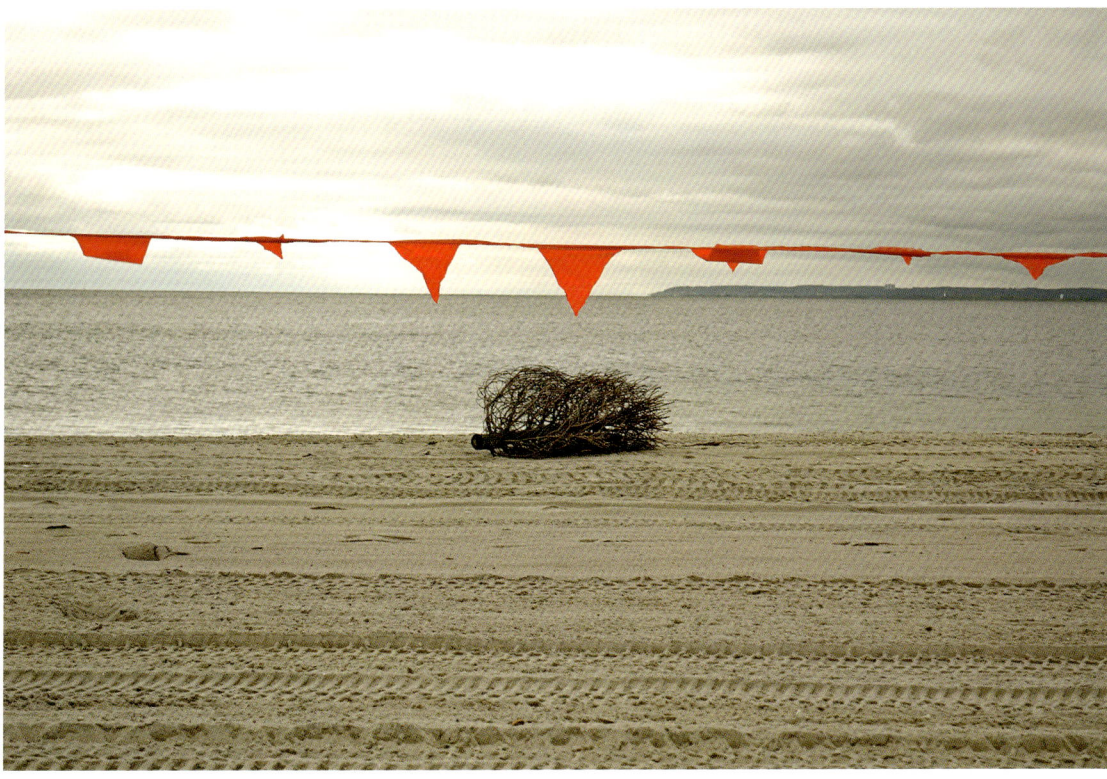

Las Vegas, Nevada

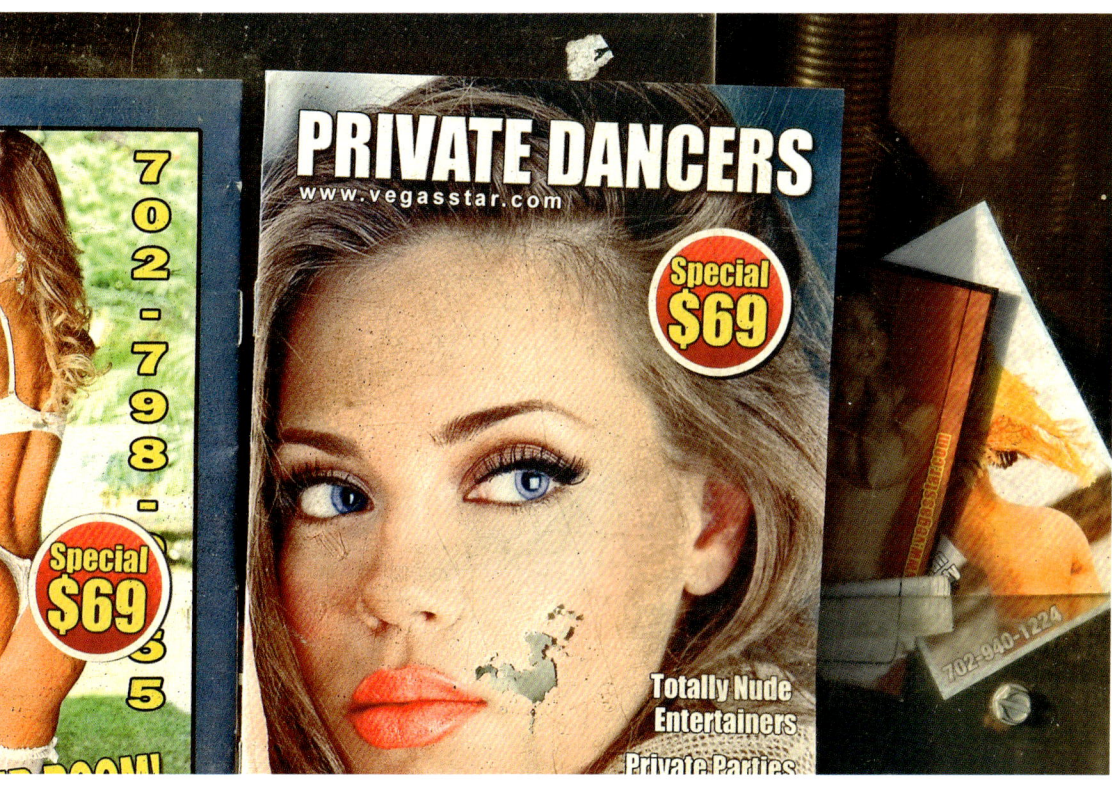

Arcadia, California

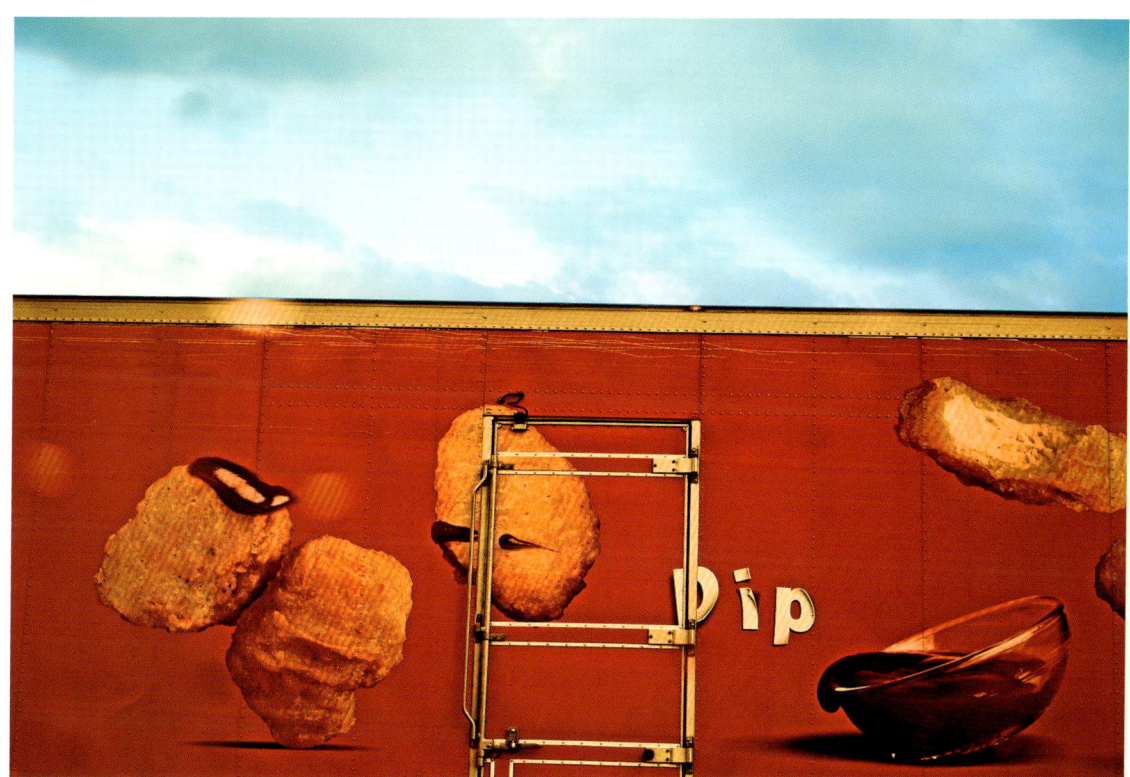

Las Vegas, Nevada

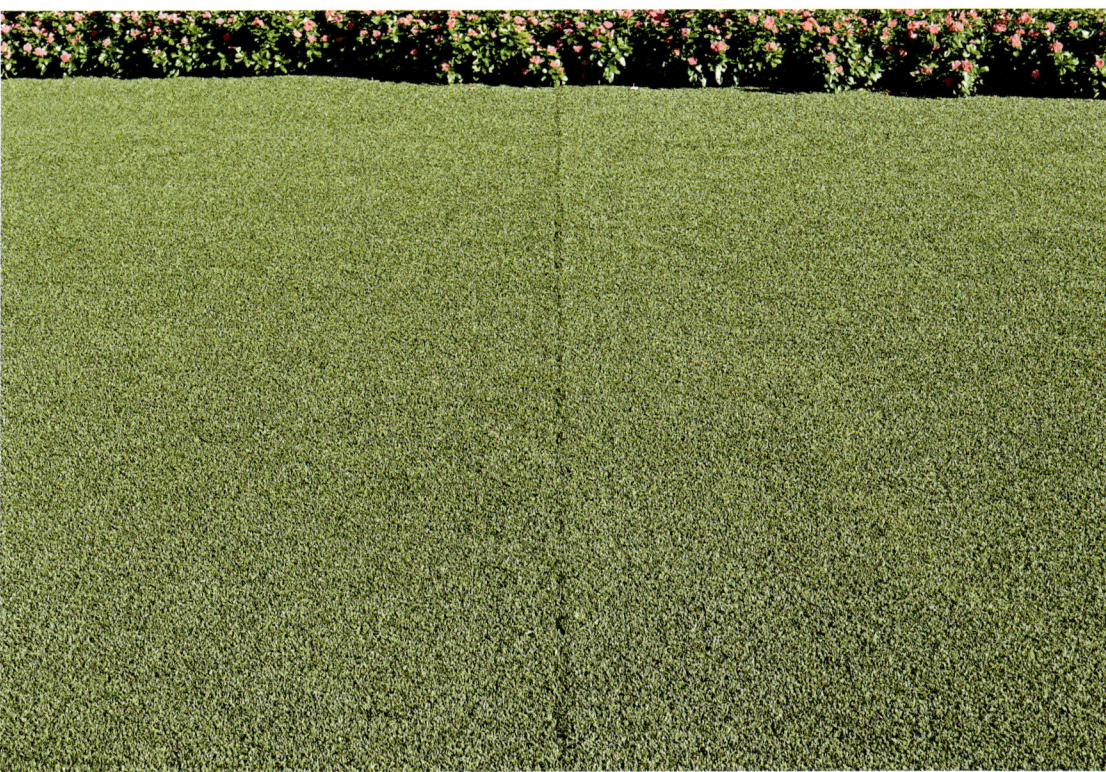

Hays, Kansas

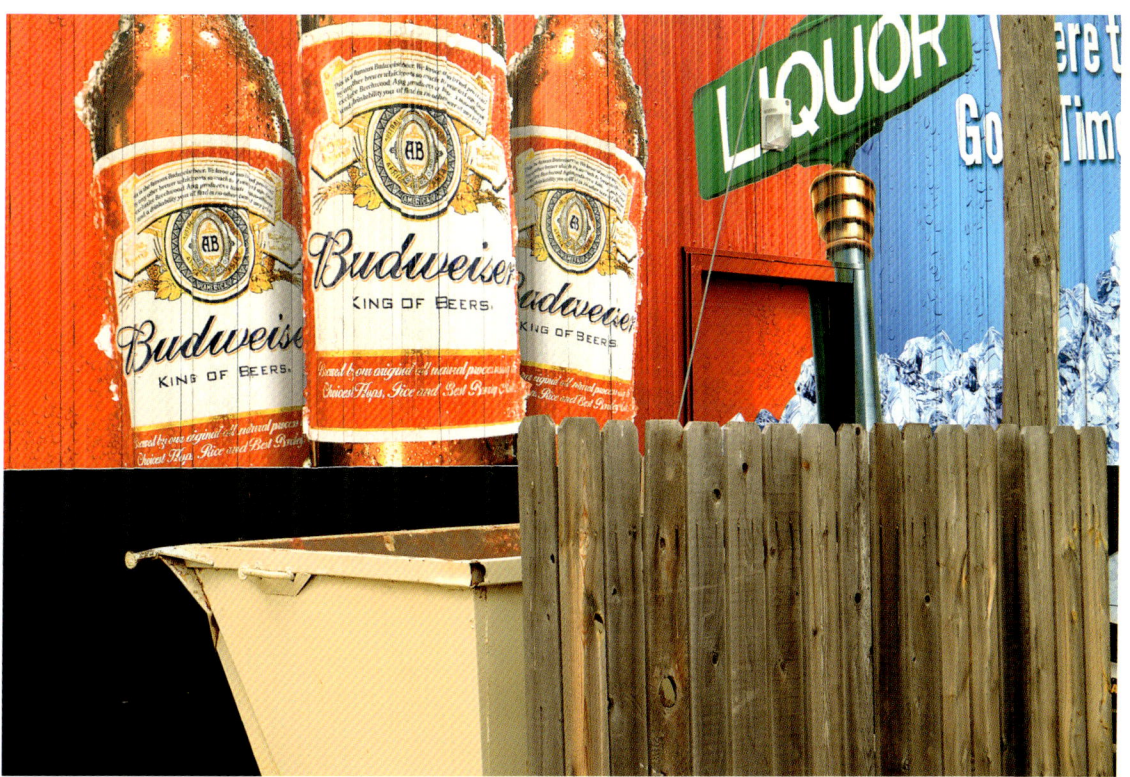

Seligman, Arizona

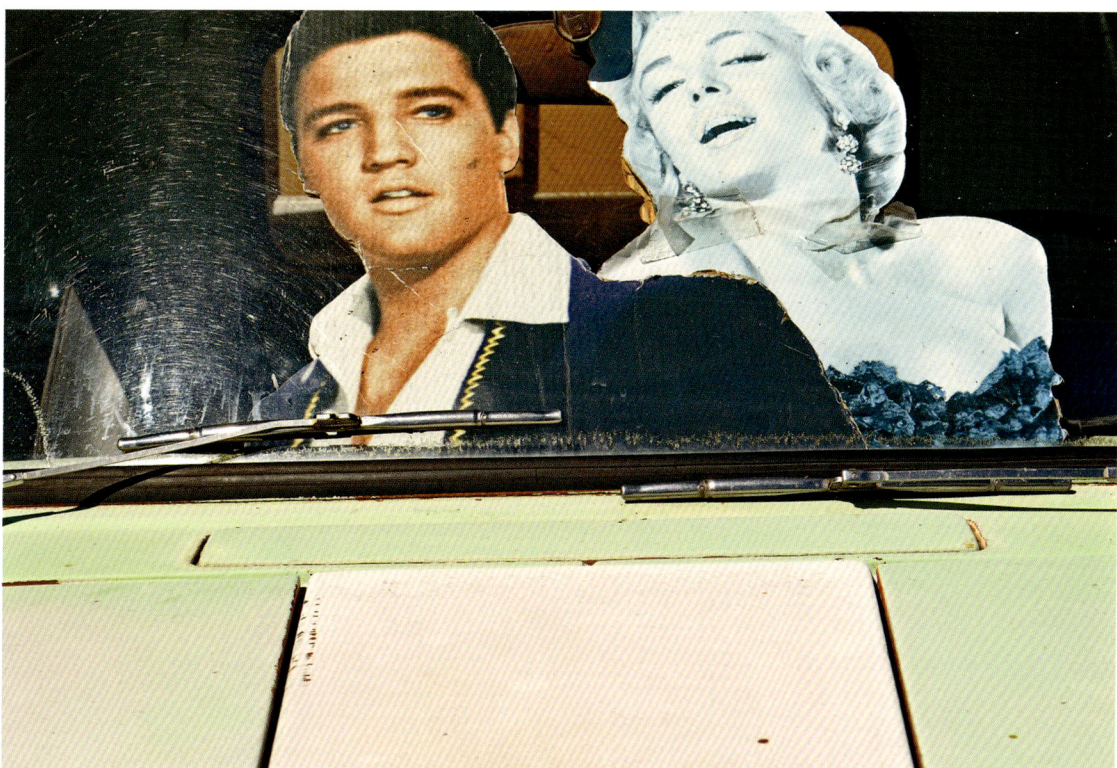

Royal Gorge, Colorado

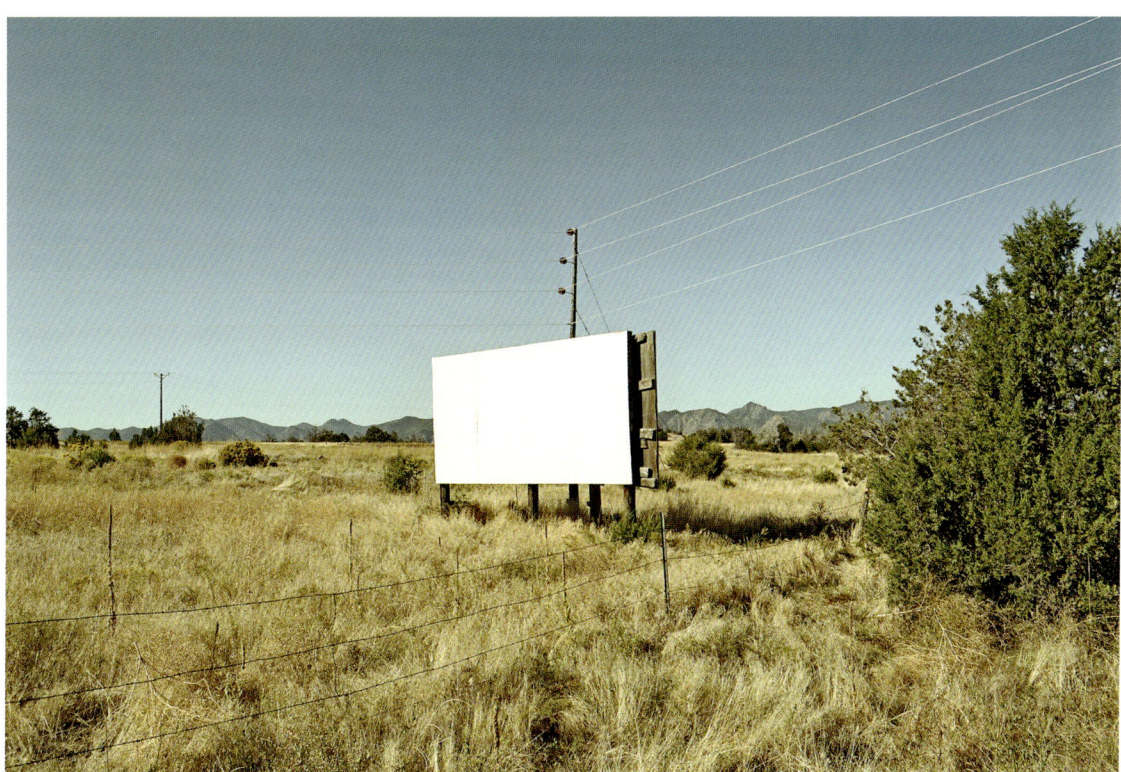

Abilene, Kansas

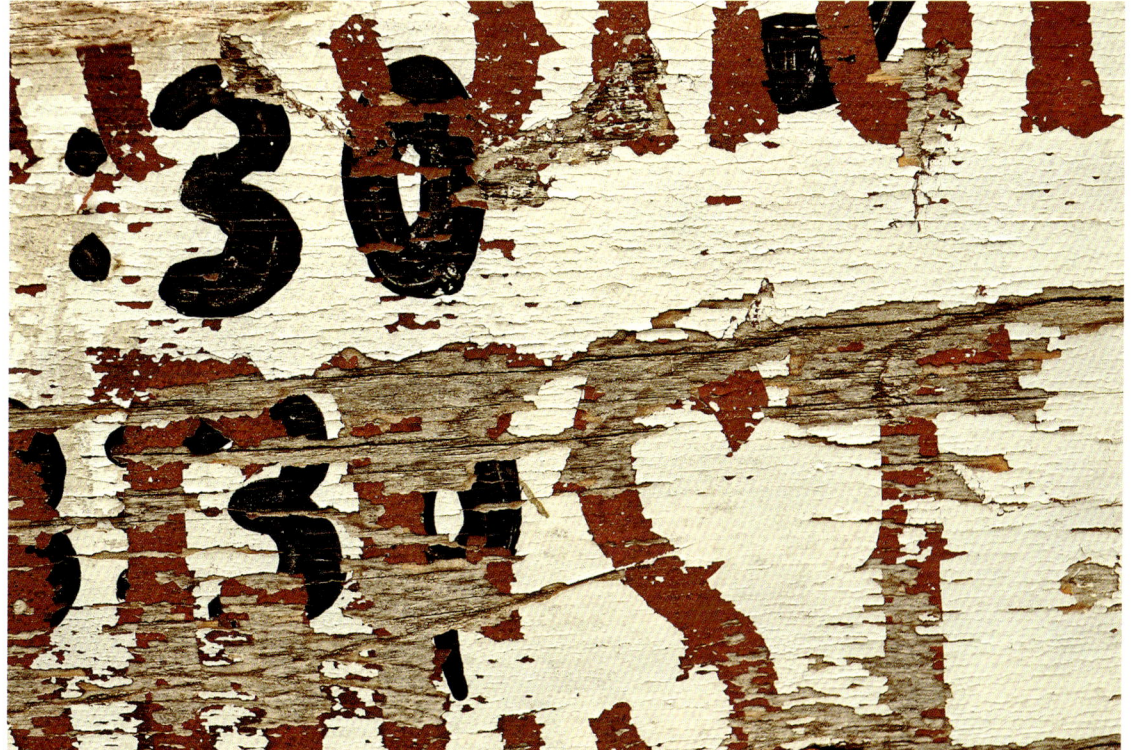

Boulder City, Nevada

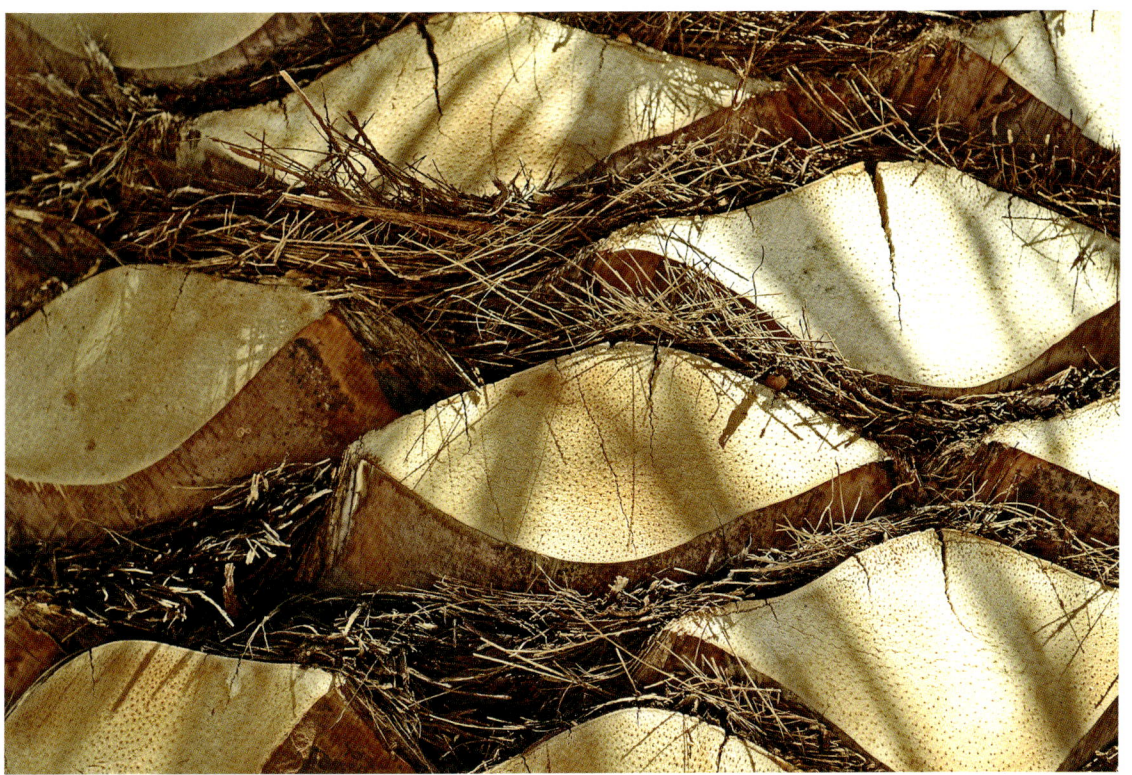

Buffalo, New York

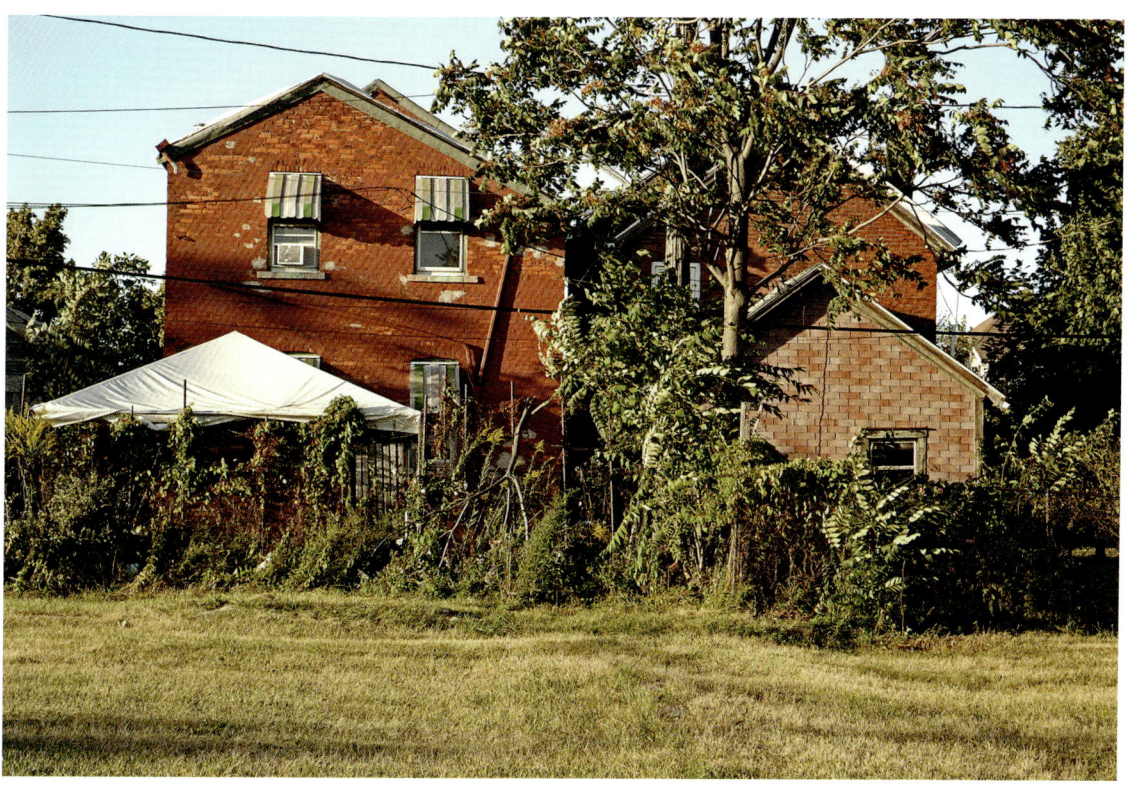

Vienna, Missouri

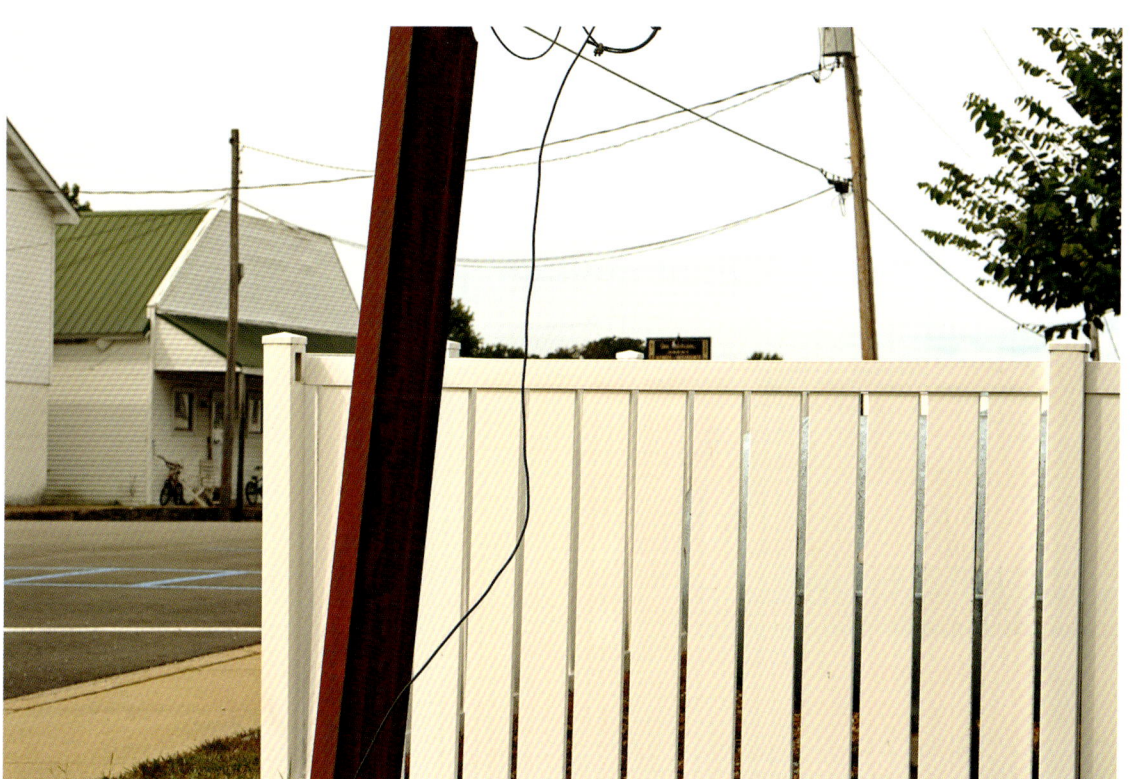

Kit Carson County, Colorado

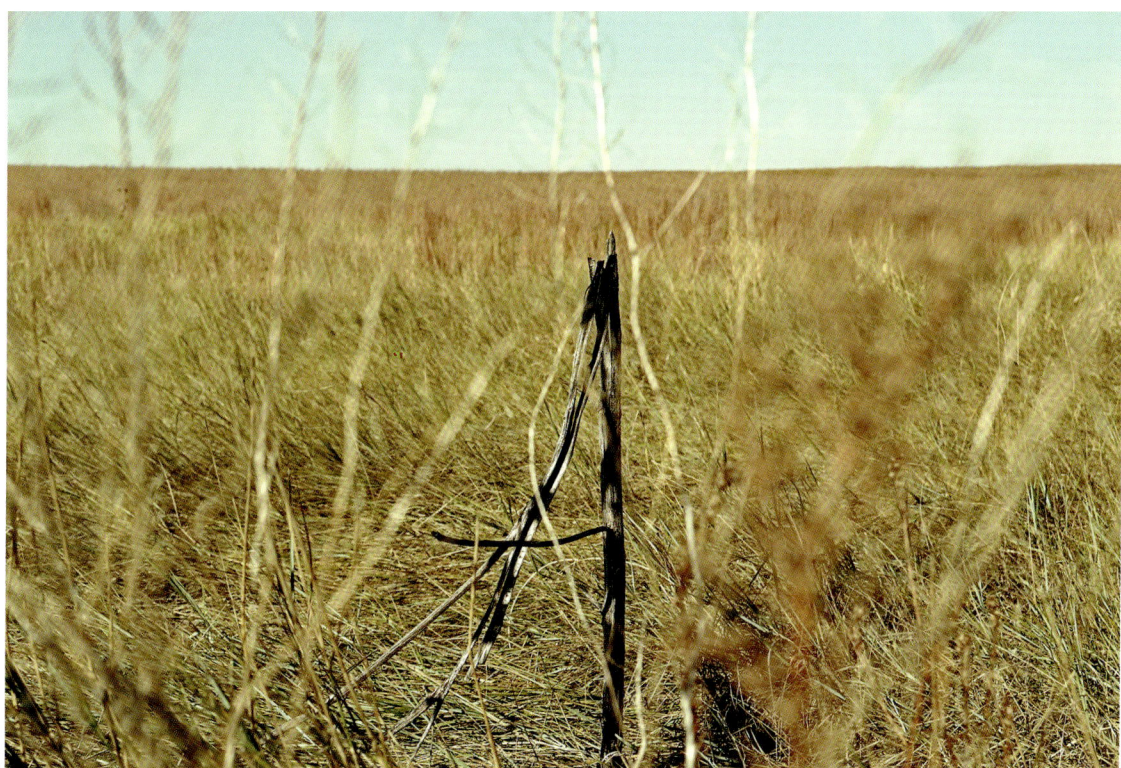

Abilene, Kansas

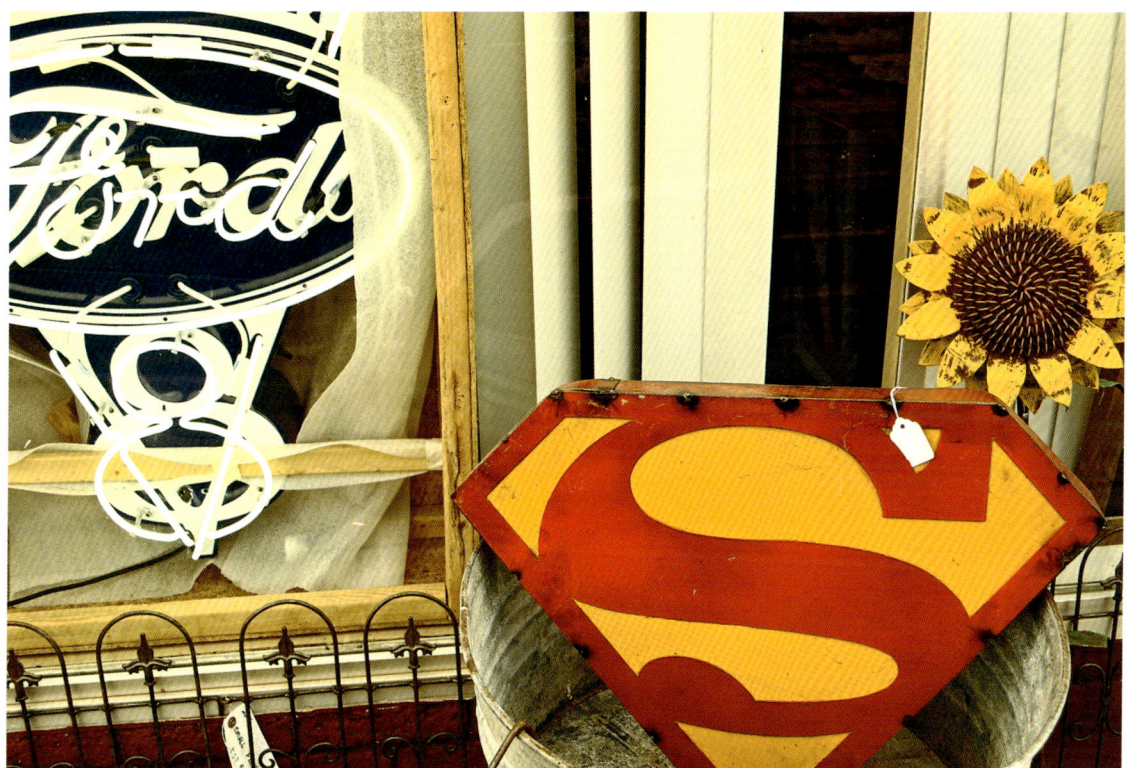

Coney Island, New York

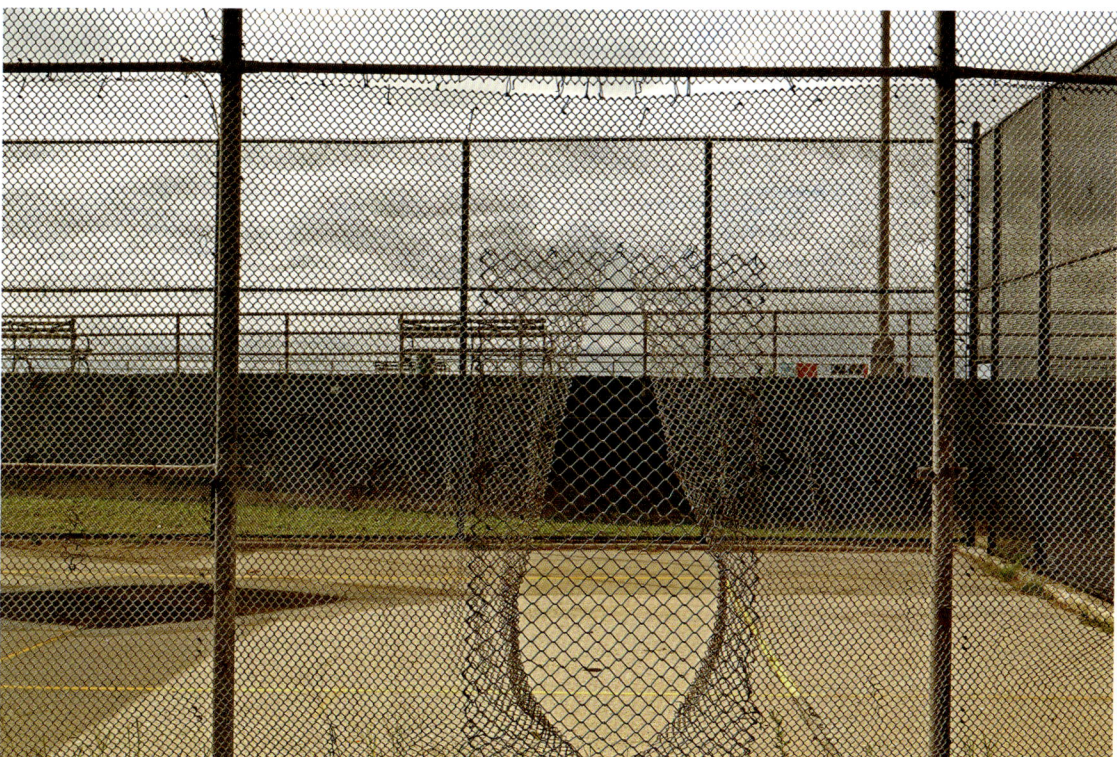

Chicago, Illinois

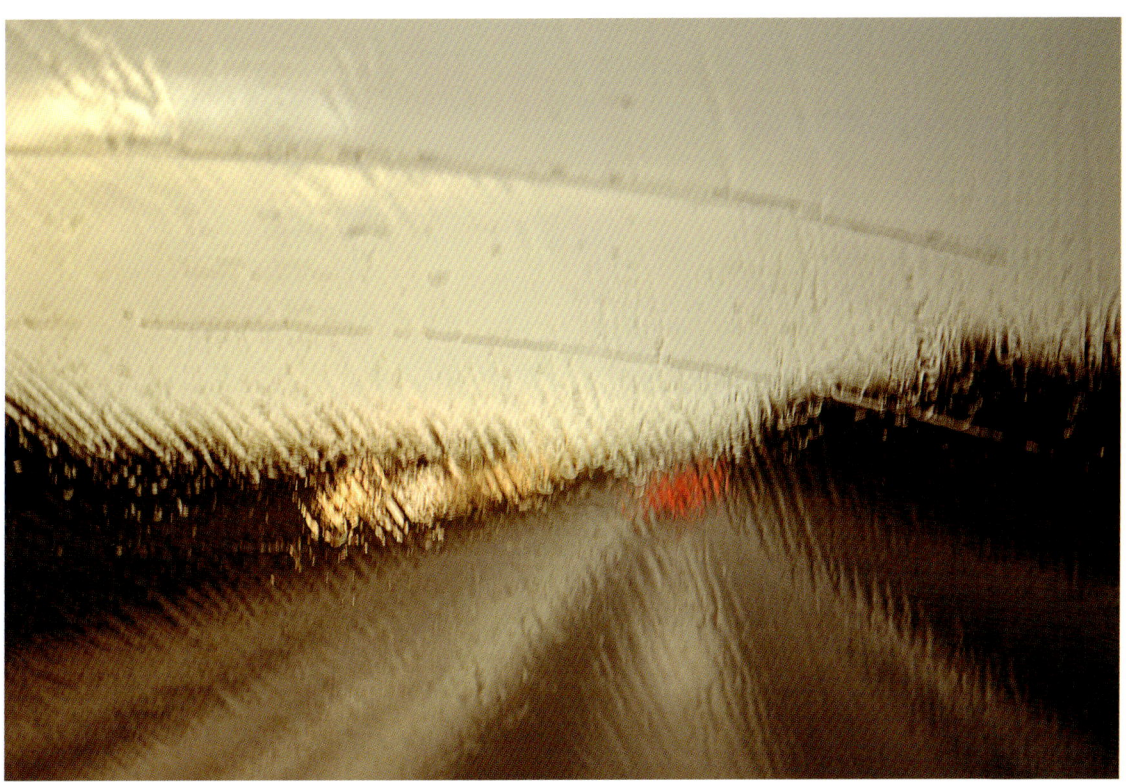

Flagstaff, Arizona

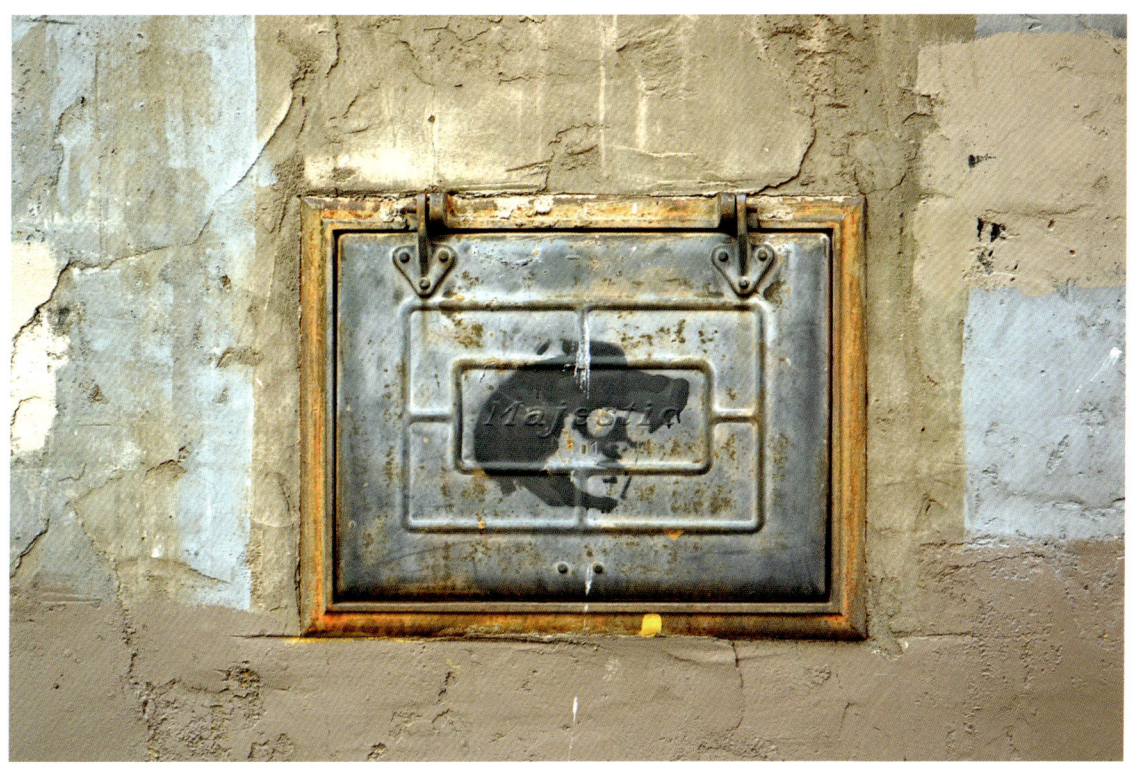

Hollywood, California

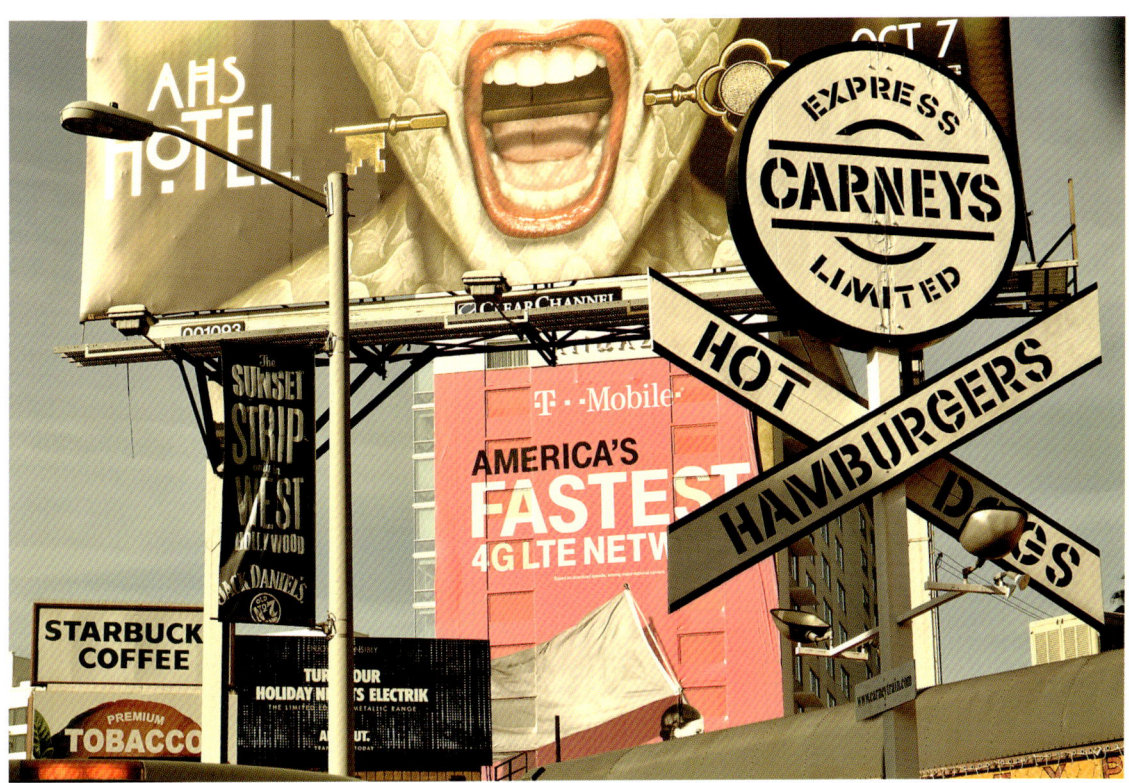

Queens, New York

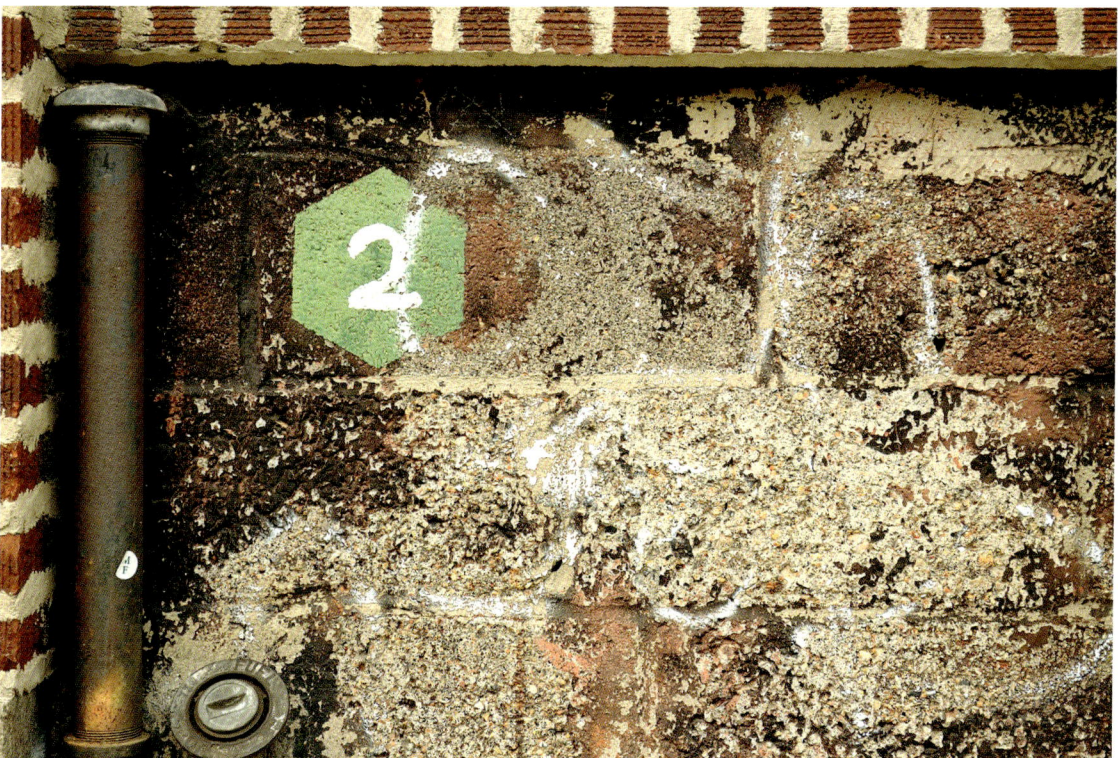

Syracuse, Missouri

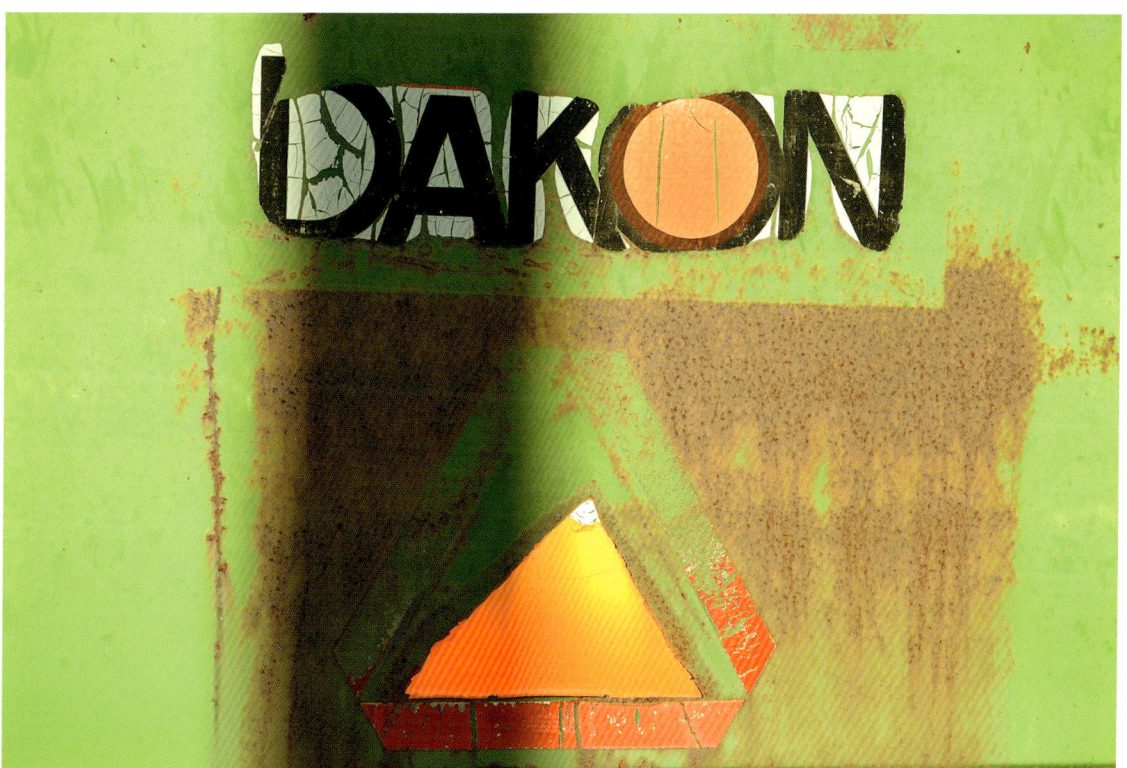

Española, New Mexico

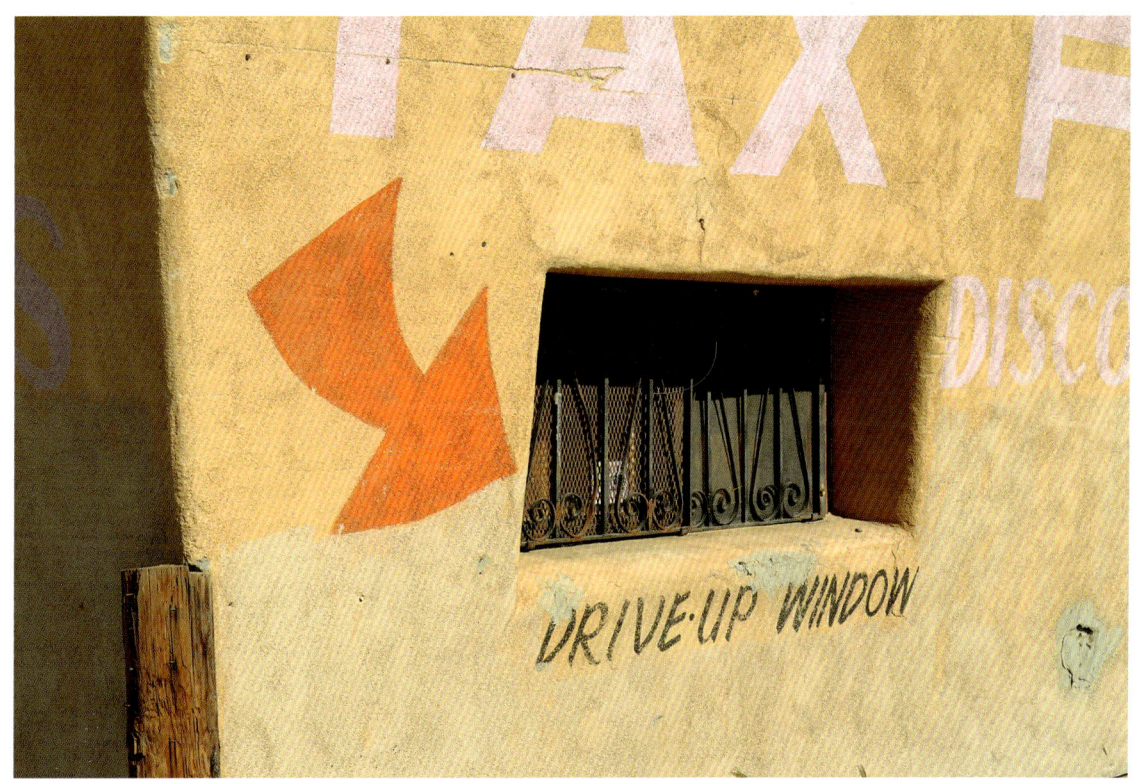

Chicago, Illinois

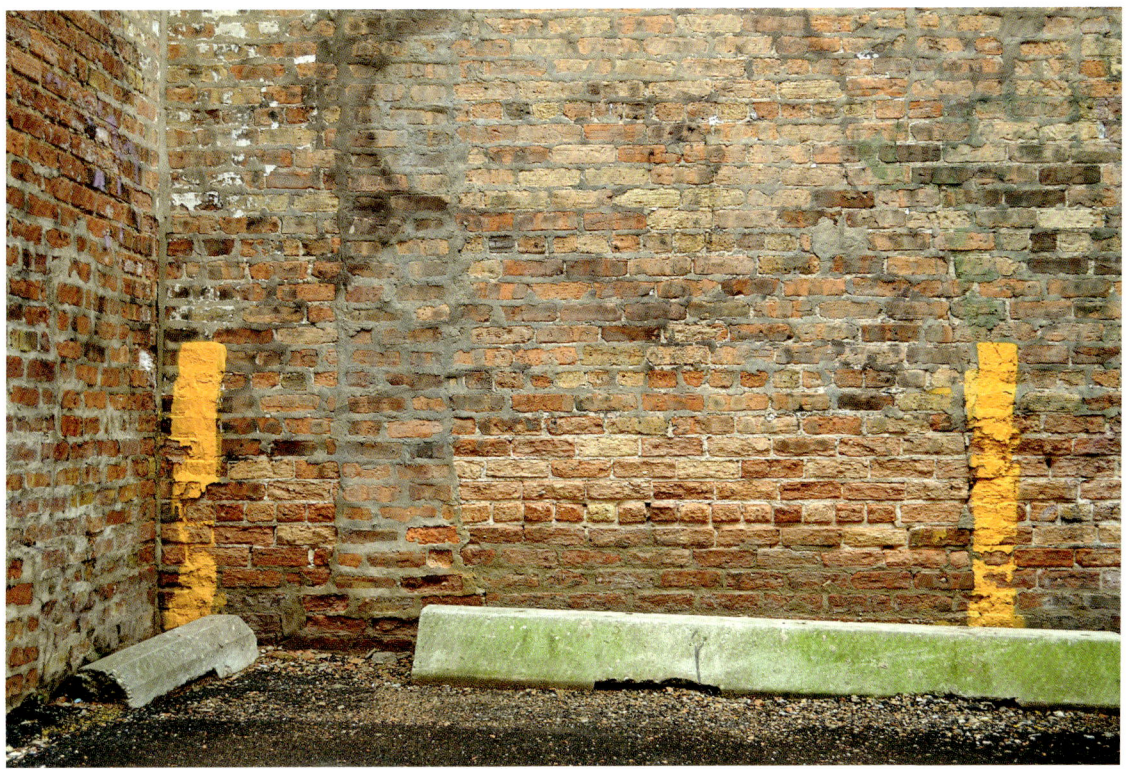

Sedalia, Missouri

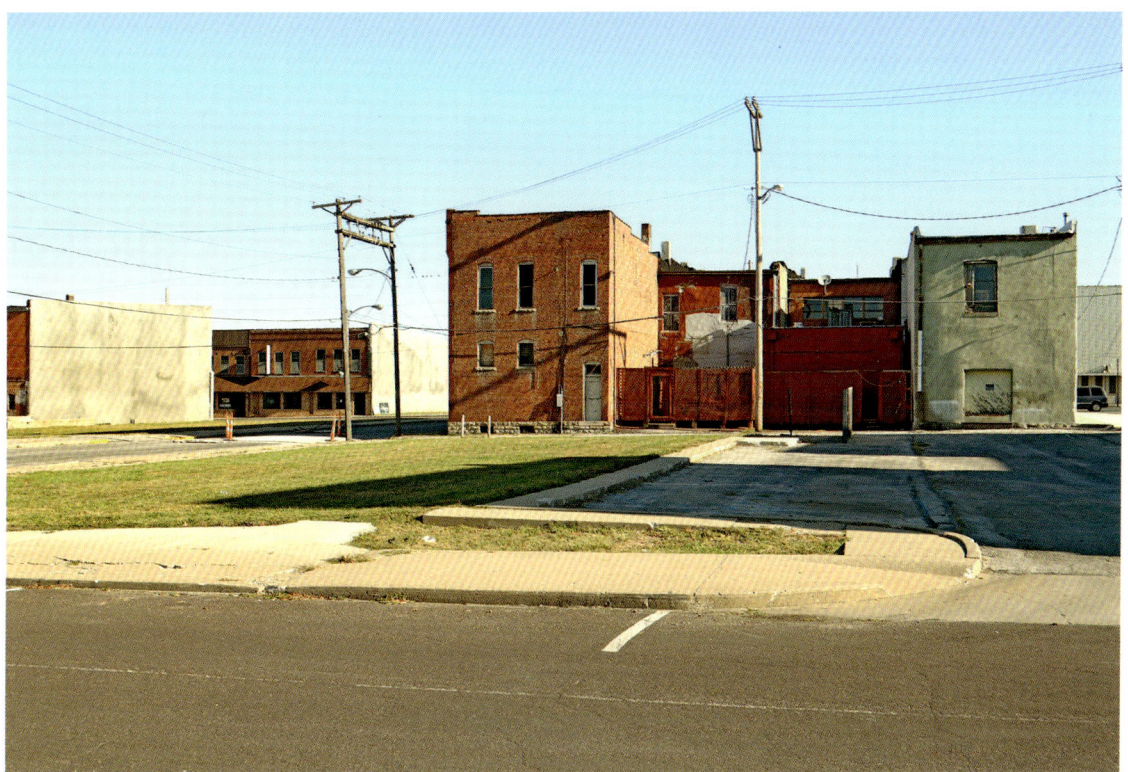

La Porte, Indiana

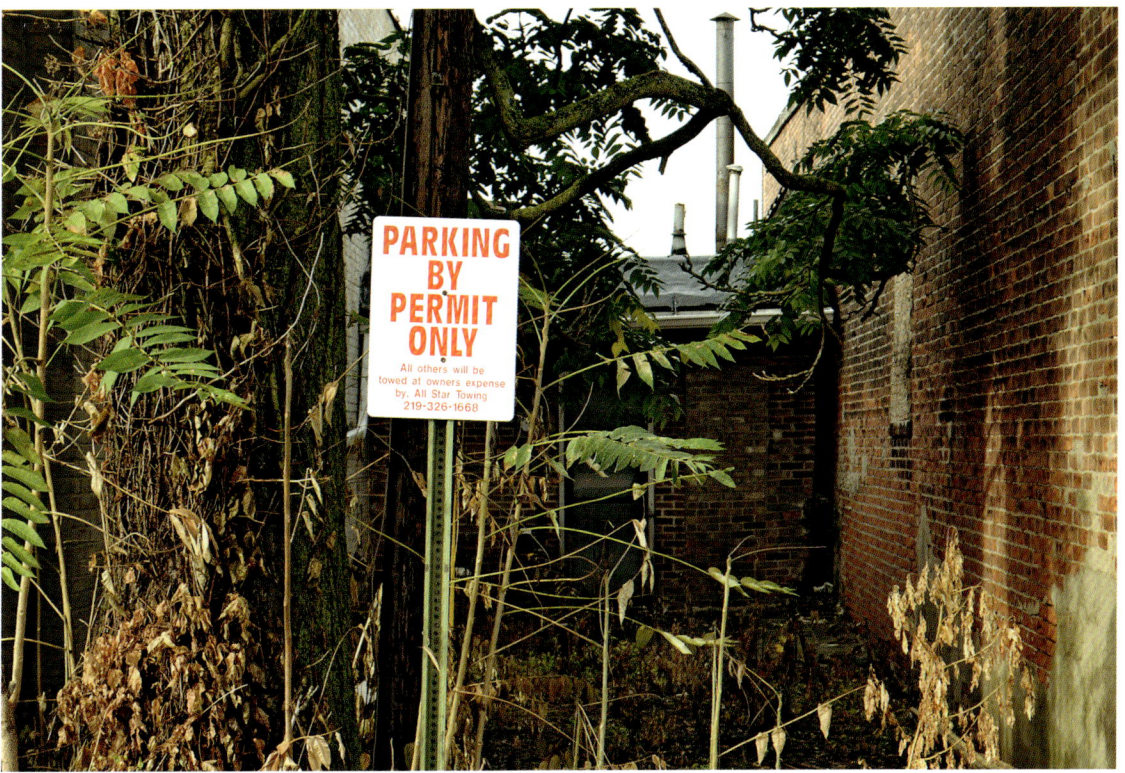

Penn Yan, New York

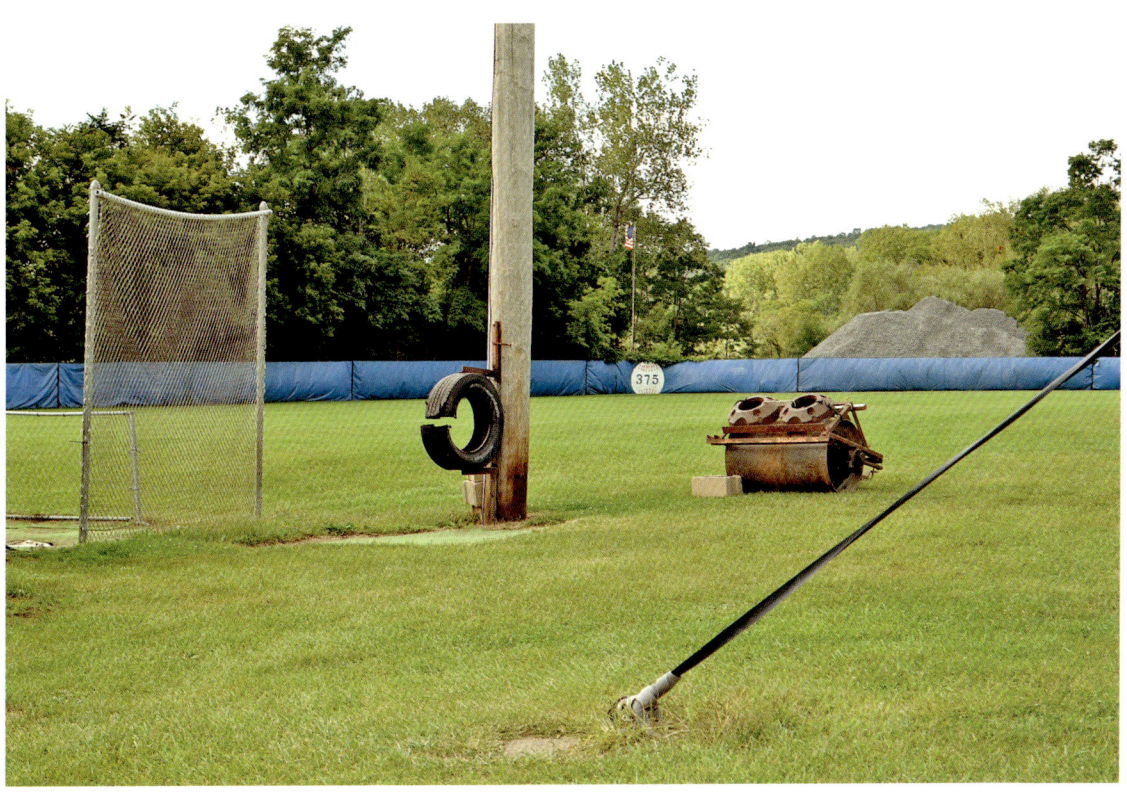

Gallup, Arizona

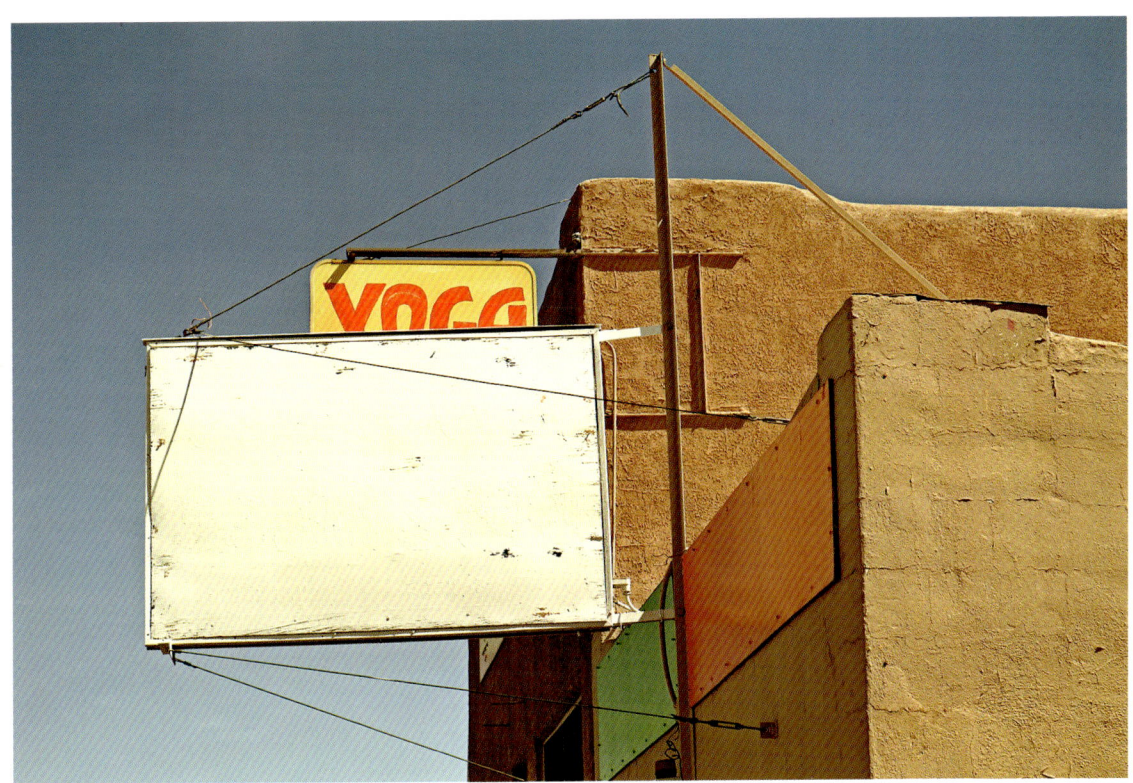

Abilene, Kansas

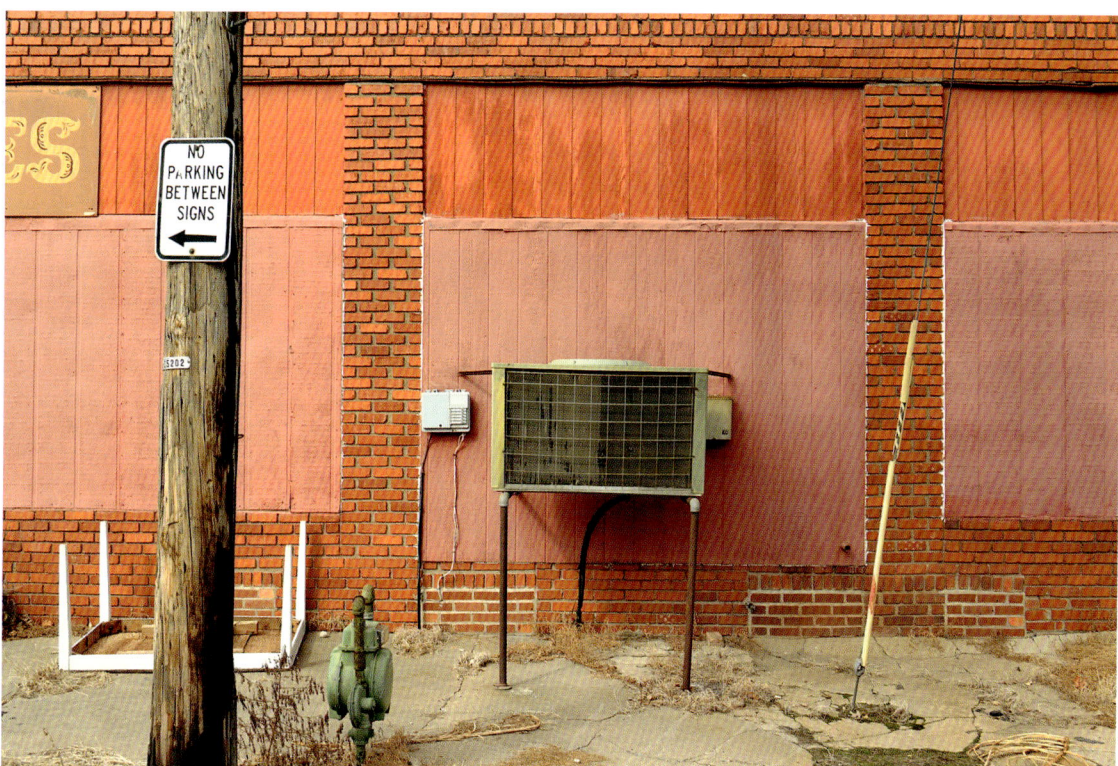

The Bronx, New York

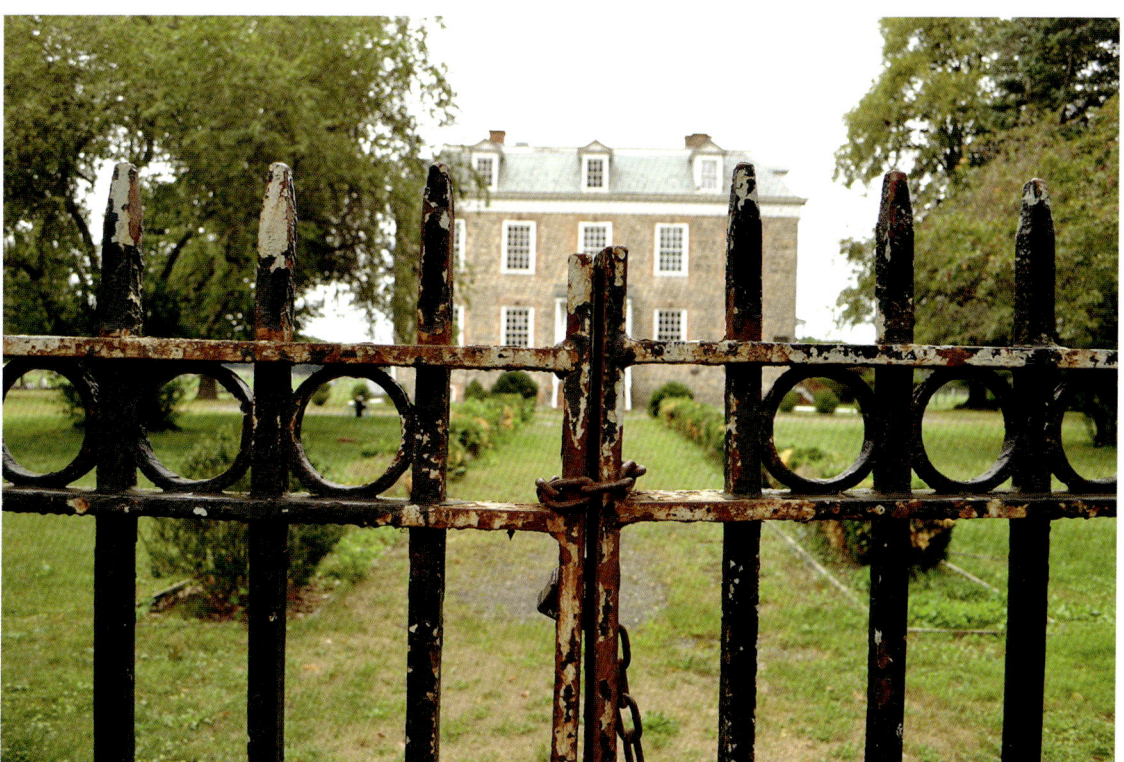

Pueblo, Colorado

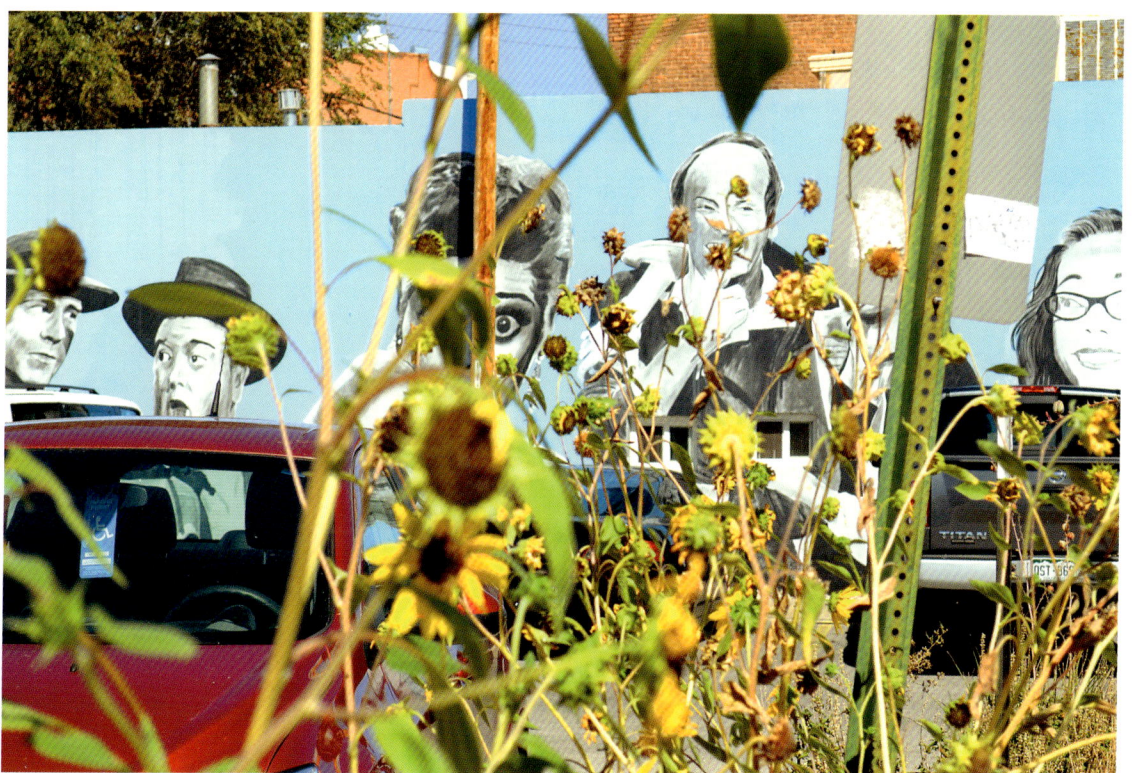

Winslow, Arizona

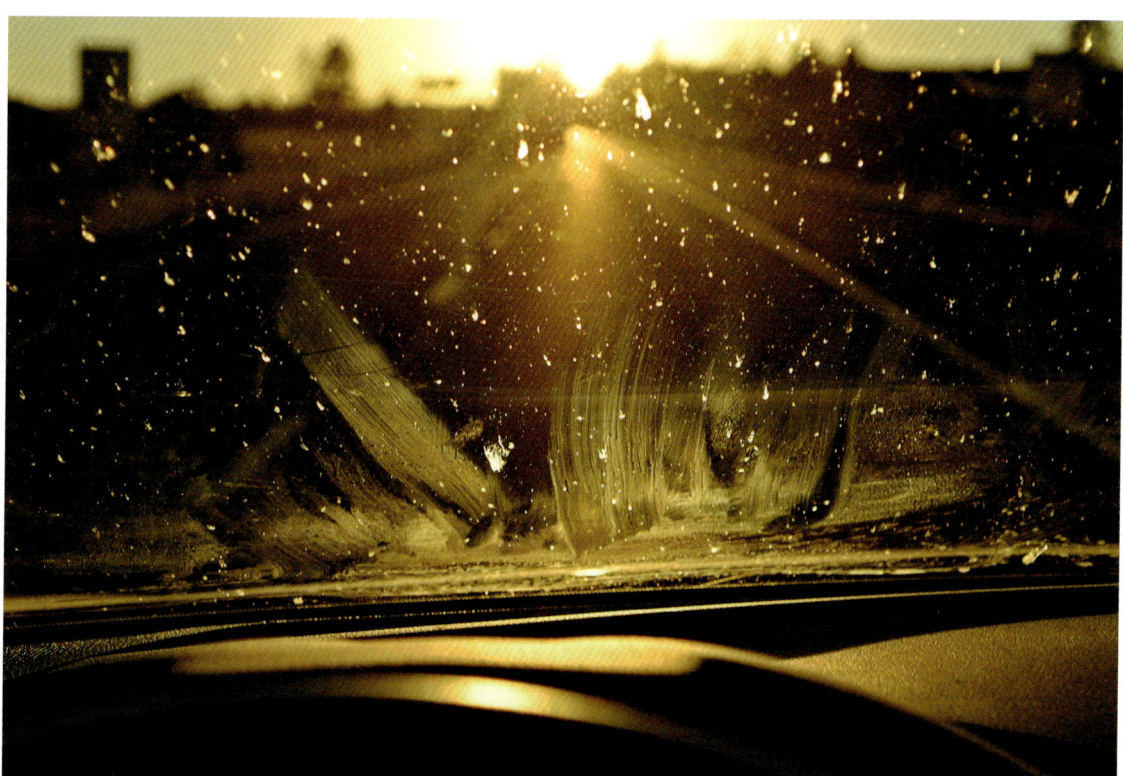

Tres Piedras, New Mexico

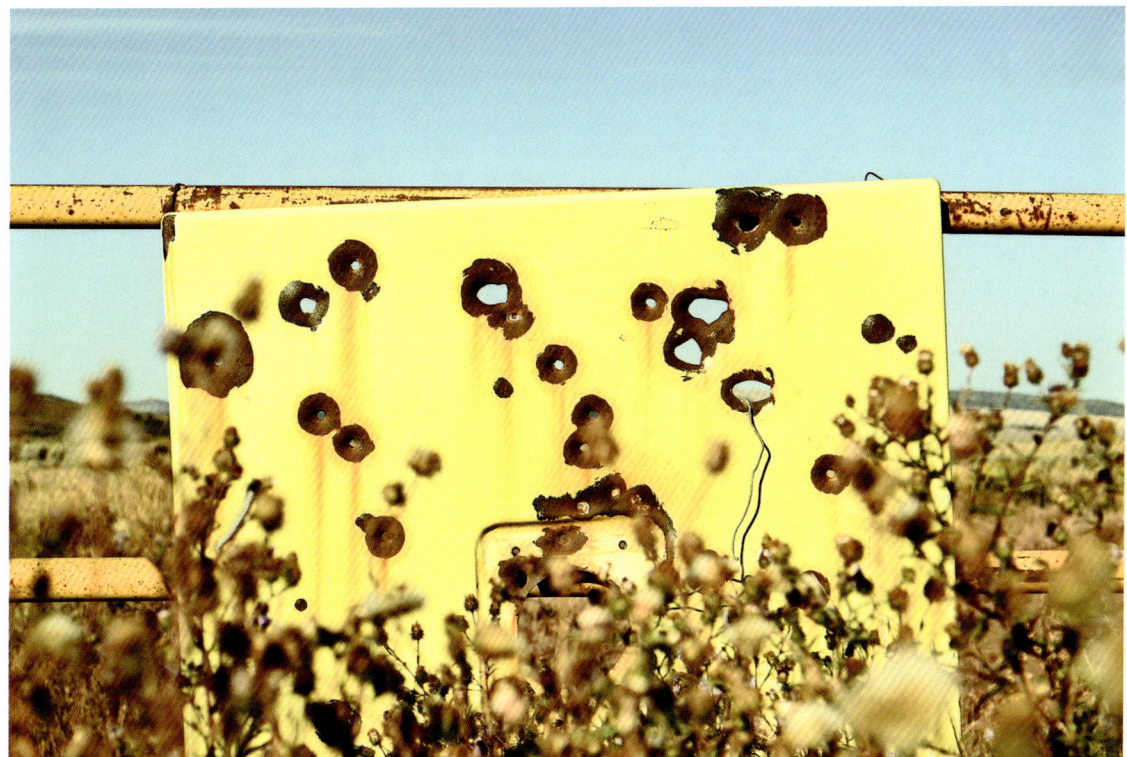

La Porte, Indiana

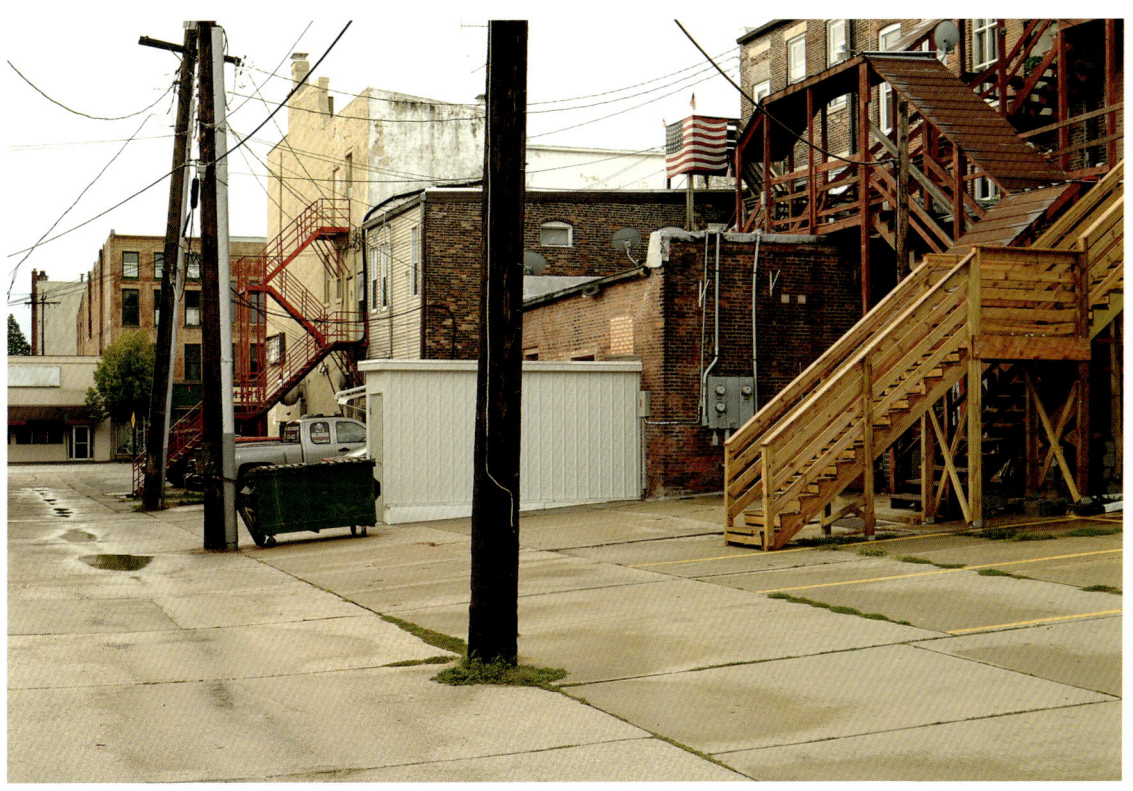

Seligman, Arizona

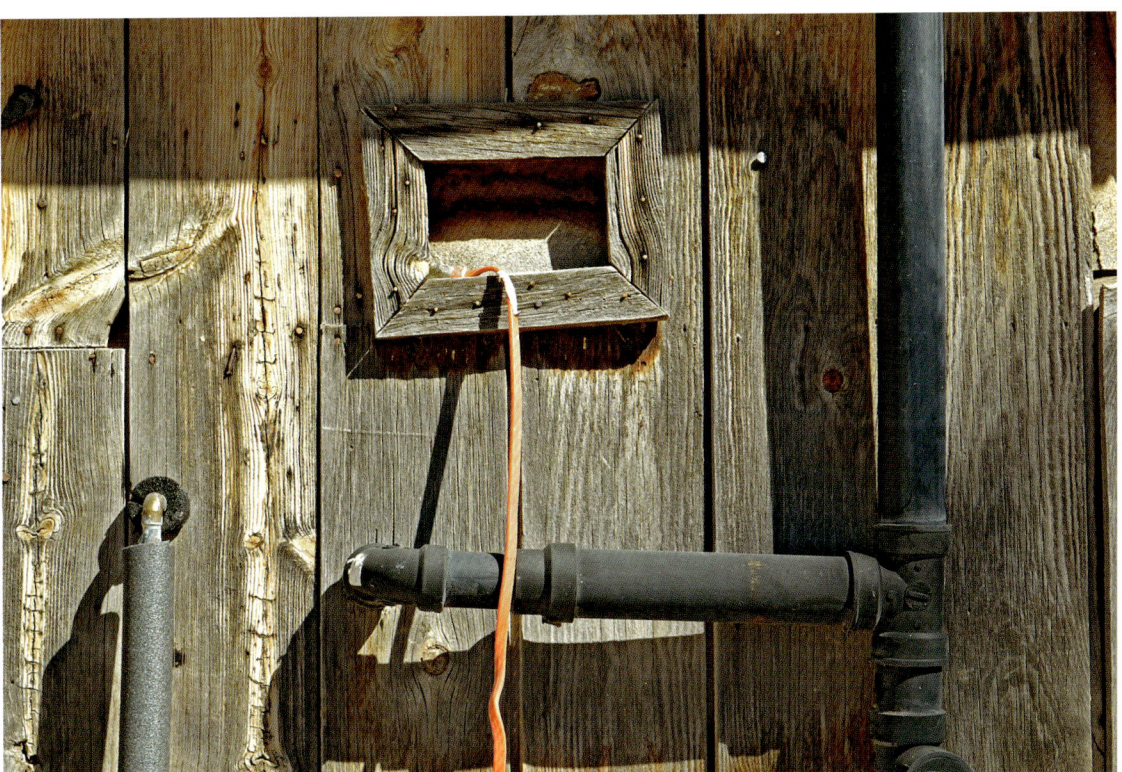

Hollywood, California

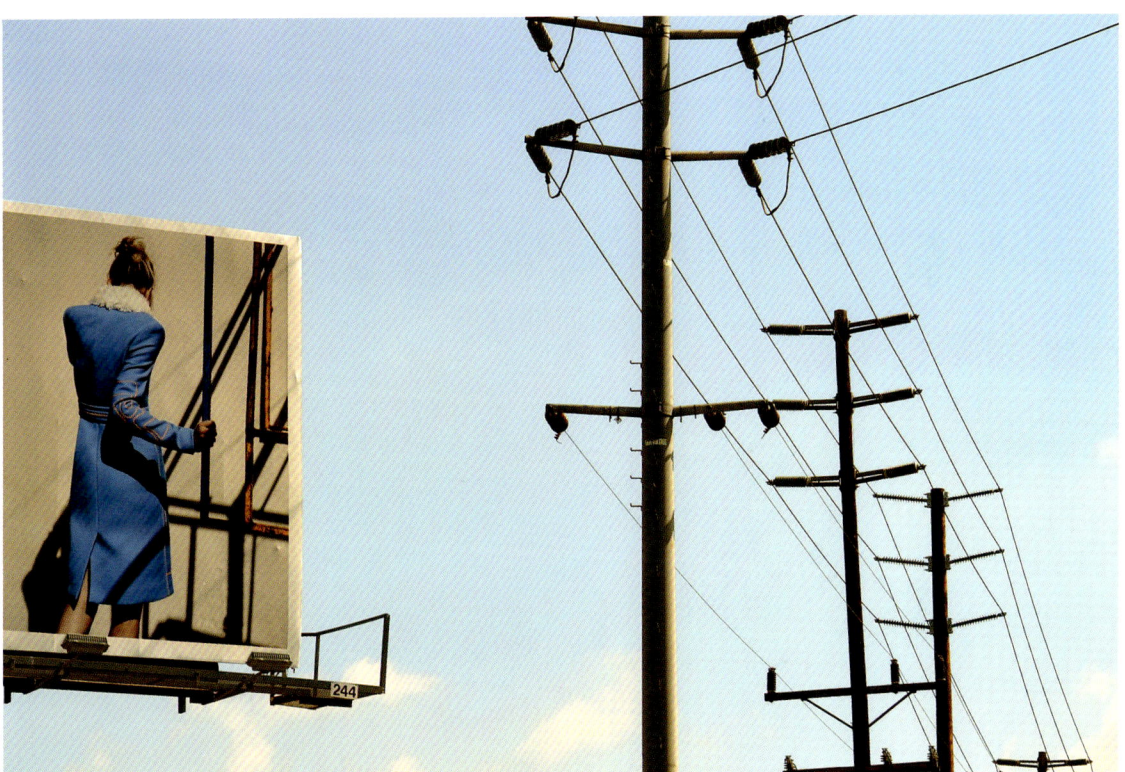

Cleveland, Ohio

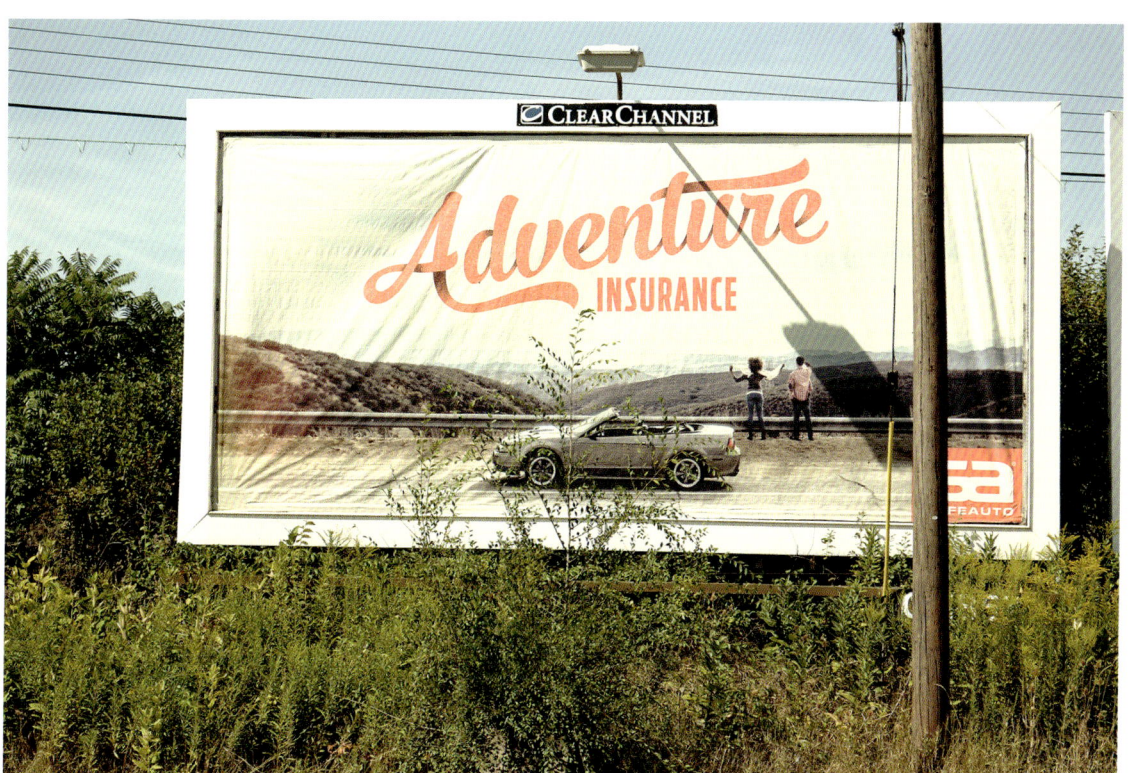

Ash Fork, Arizona

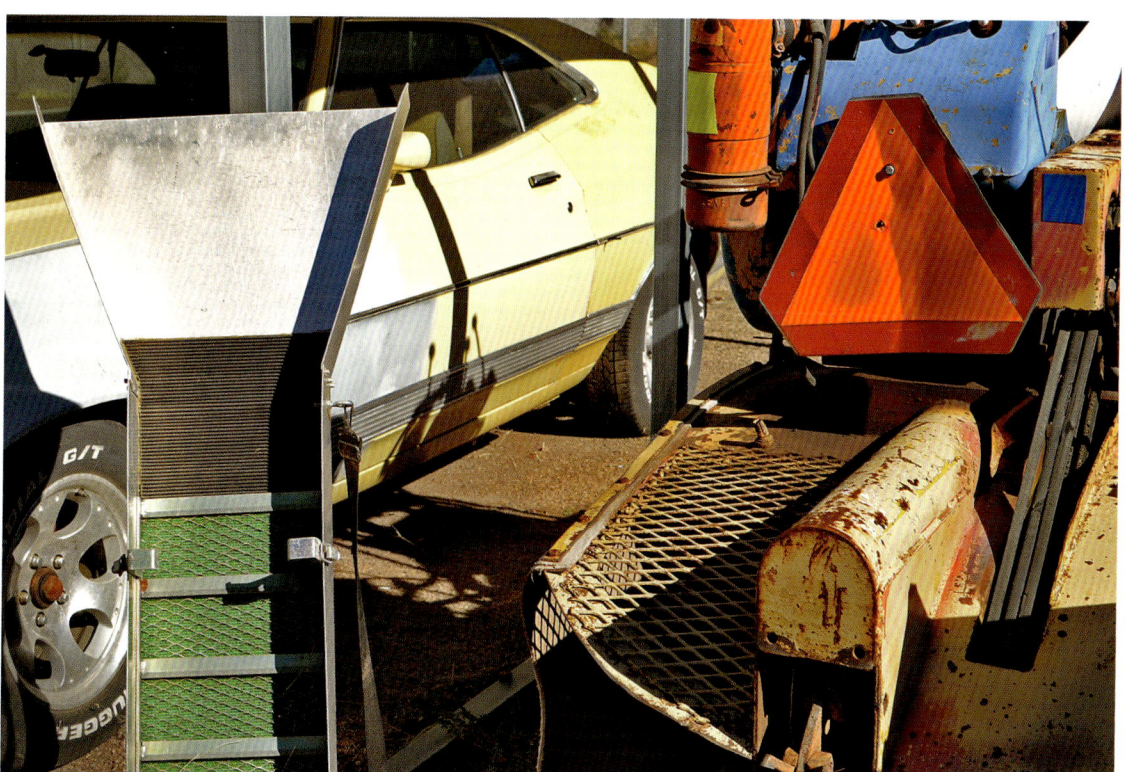

Calexico, California

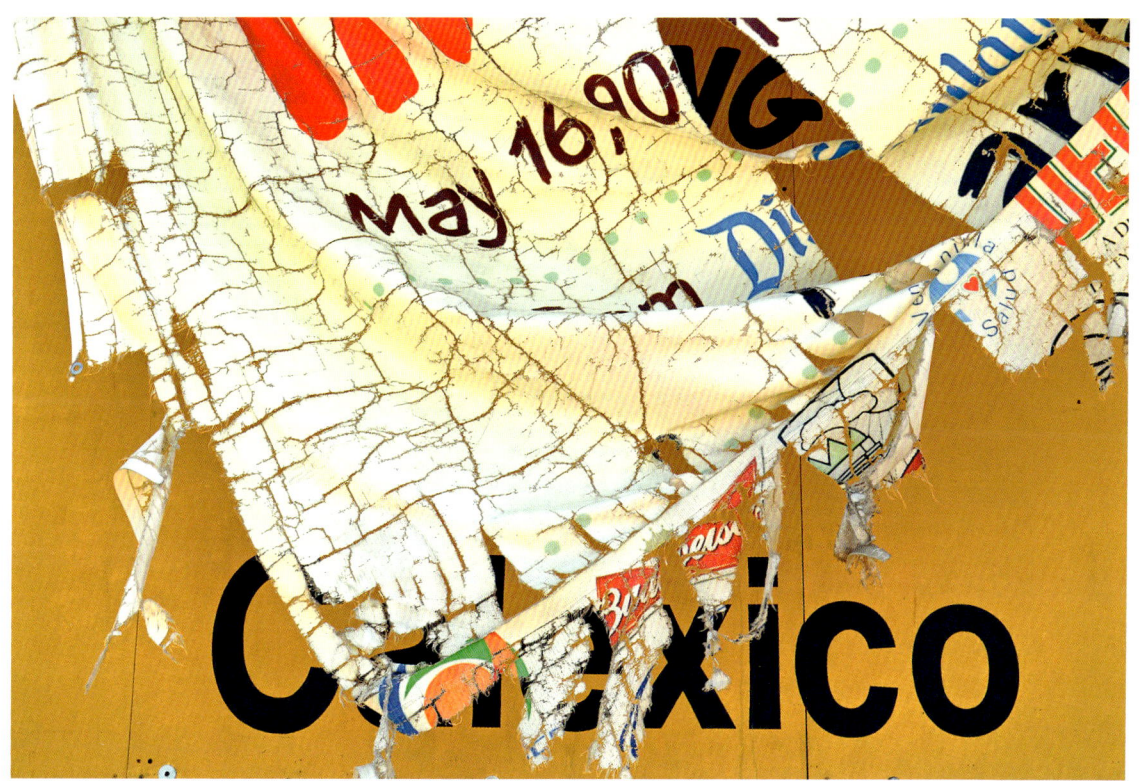

St. Joseph, Missouri

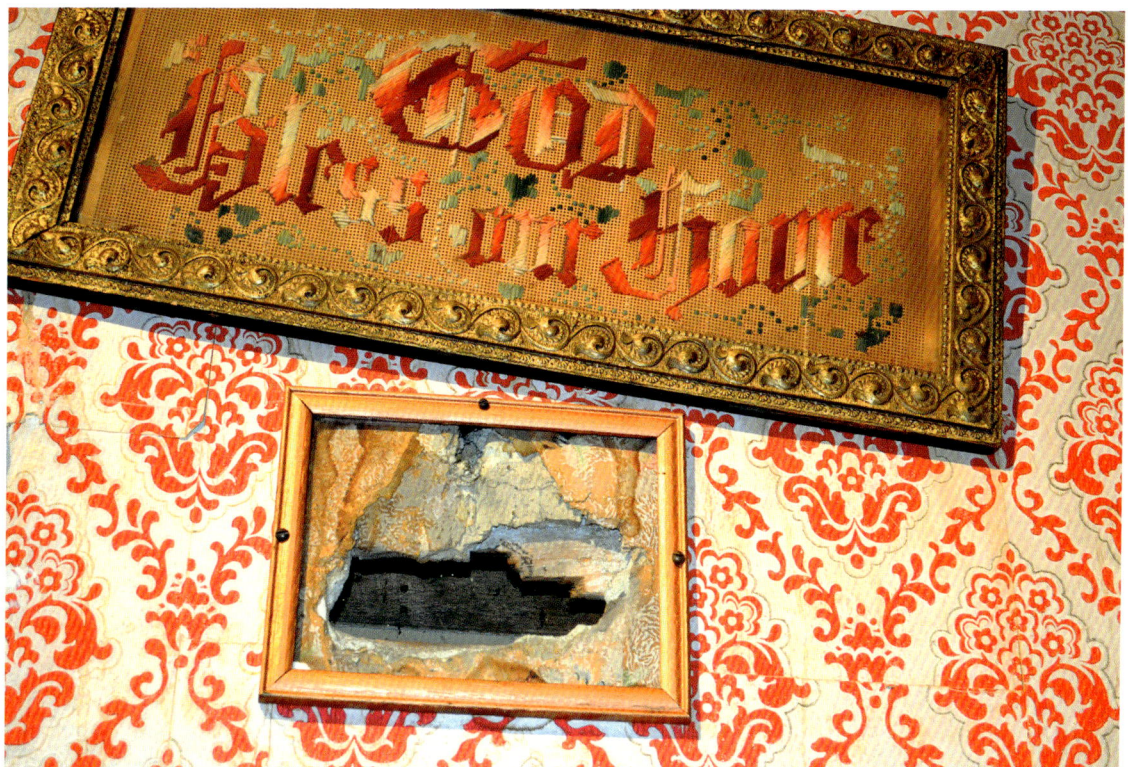

Kit Carson County, Colorado

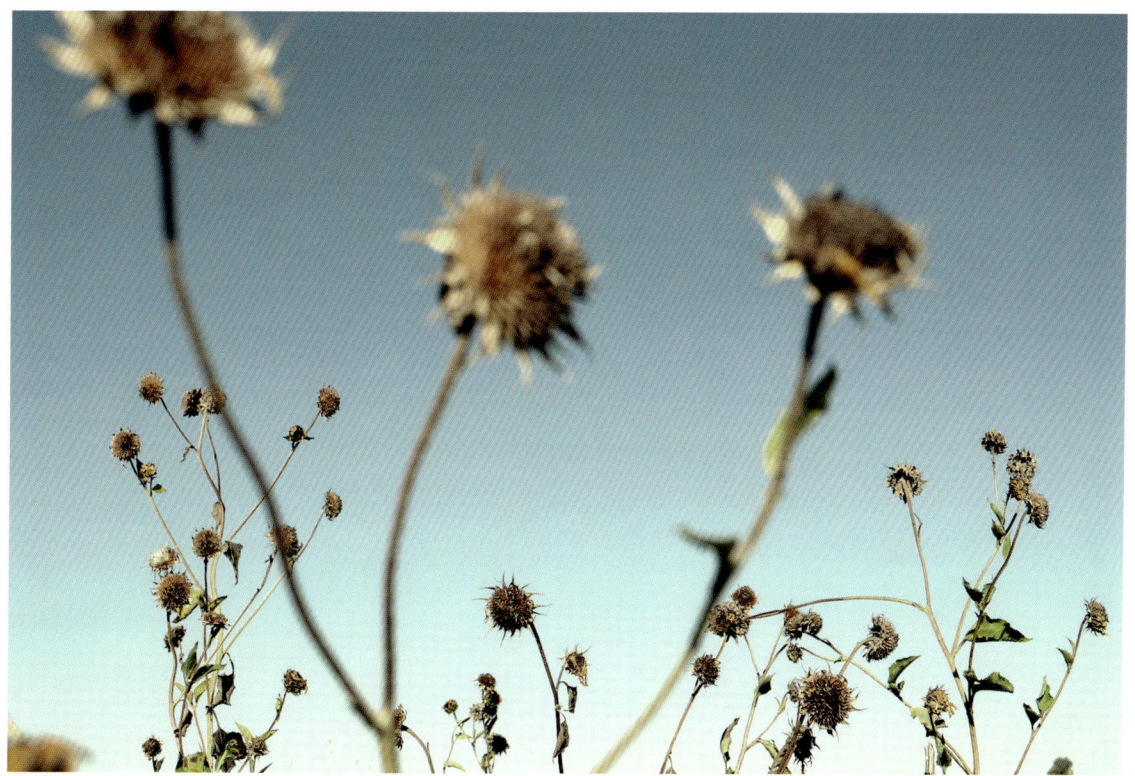

Vienna, Missouri

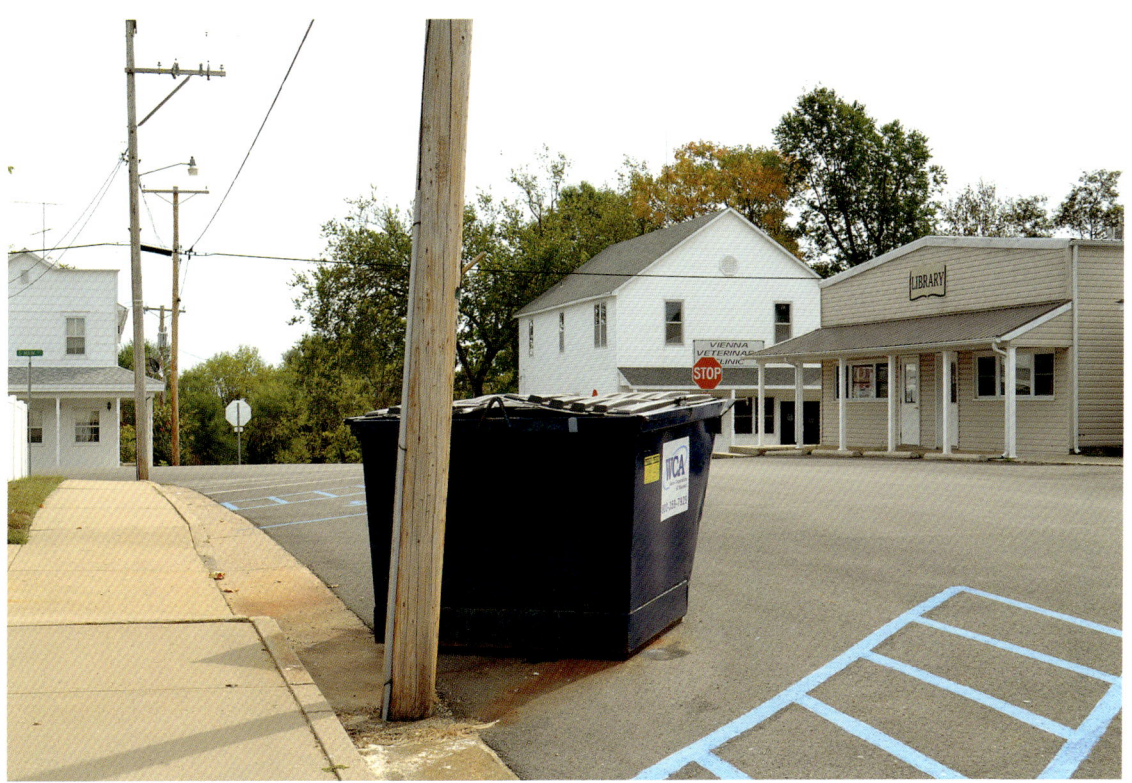

Concordia, Missouri

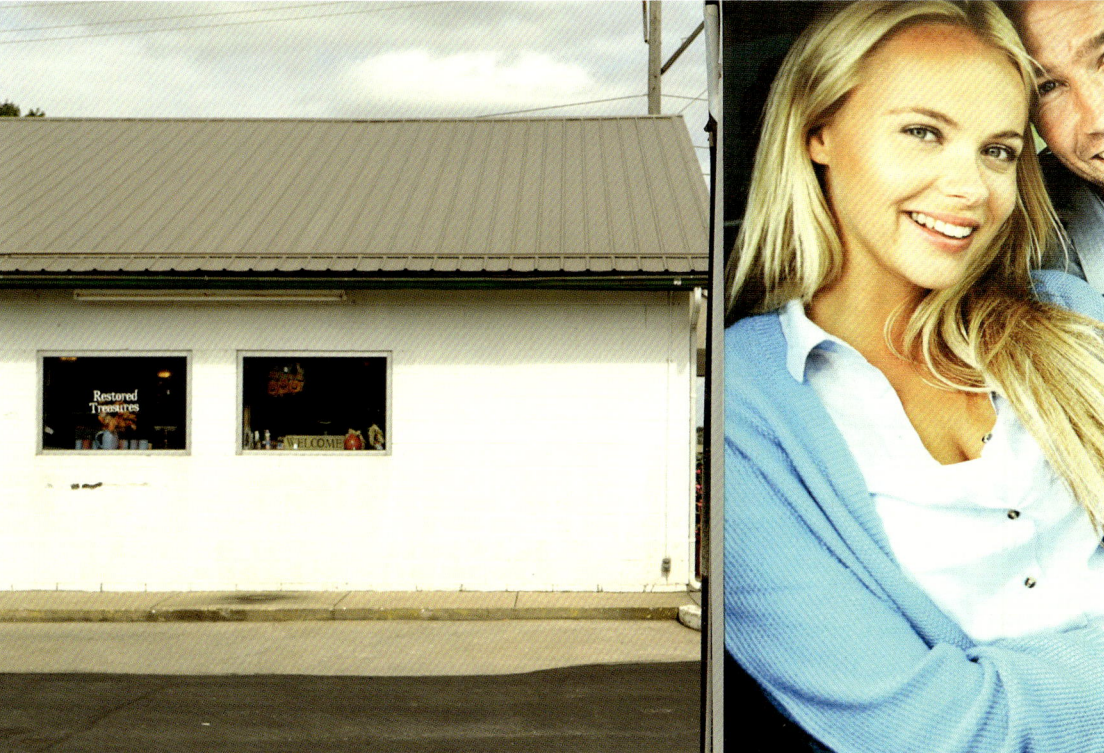

Coney Island, New York

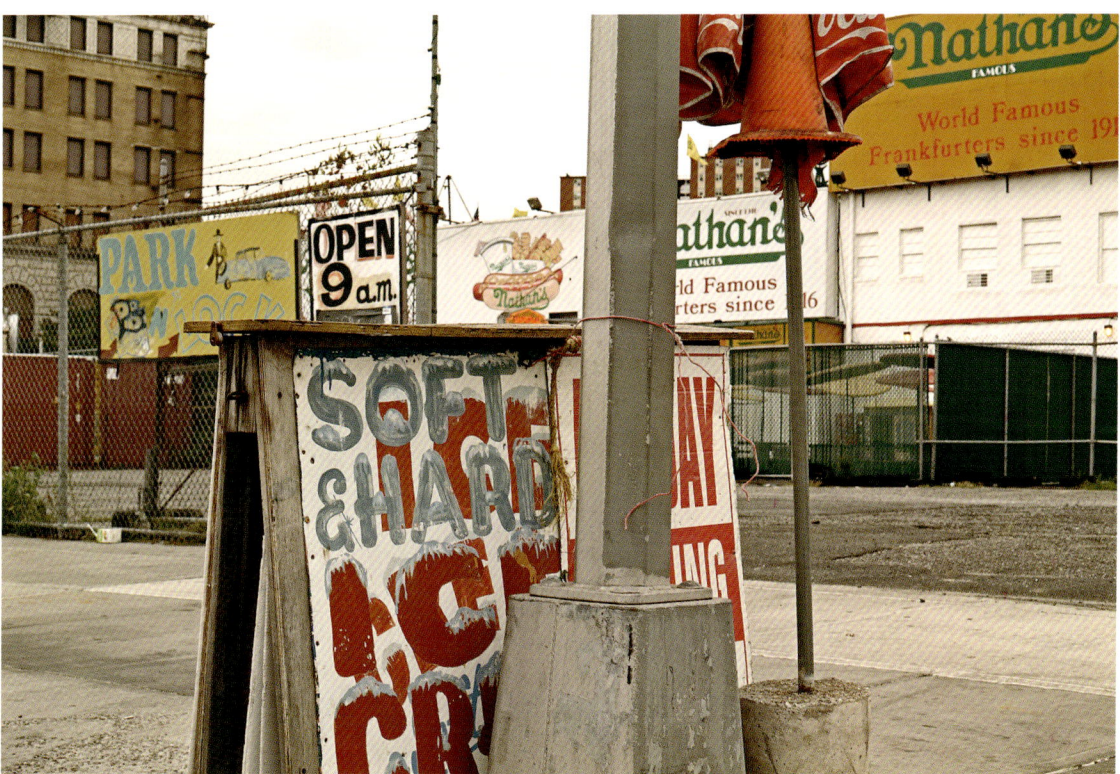

Gallup, New Mexico

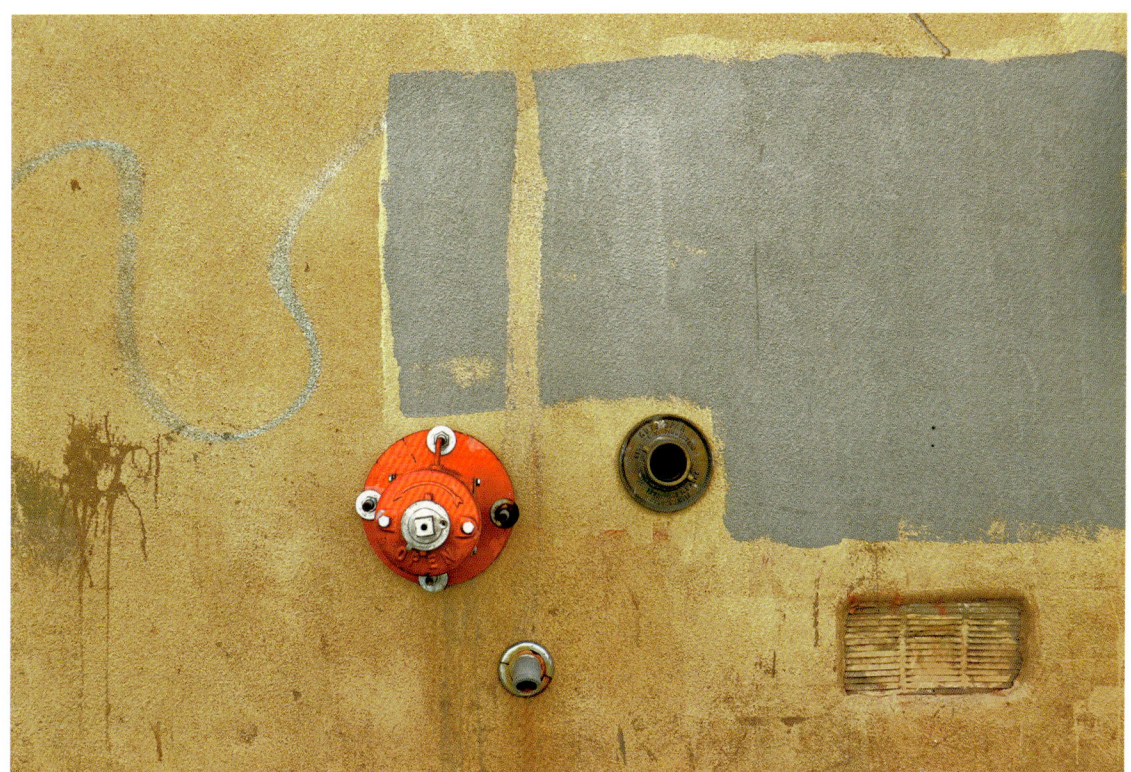

Tujunga, California

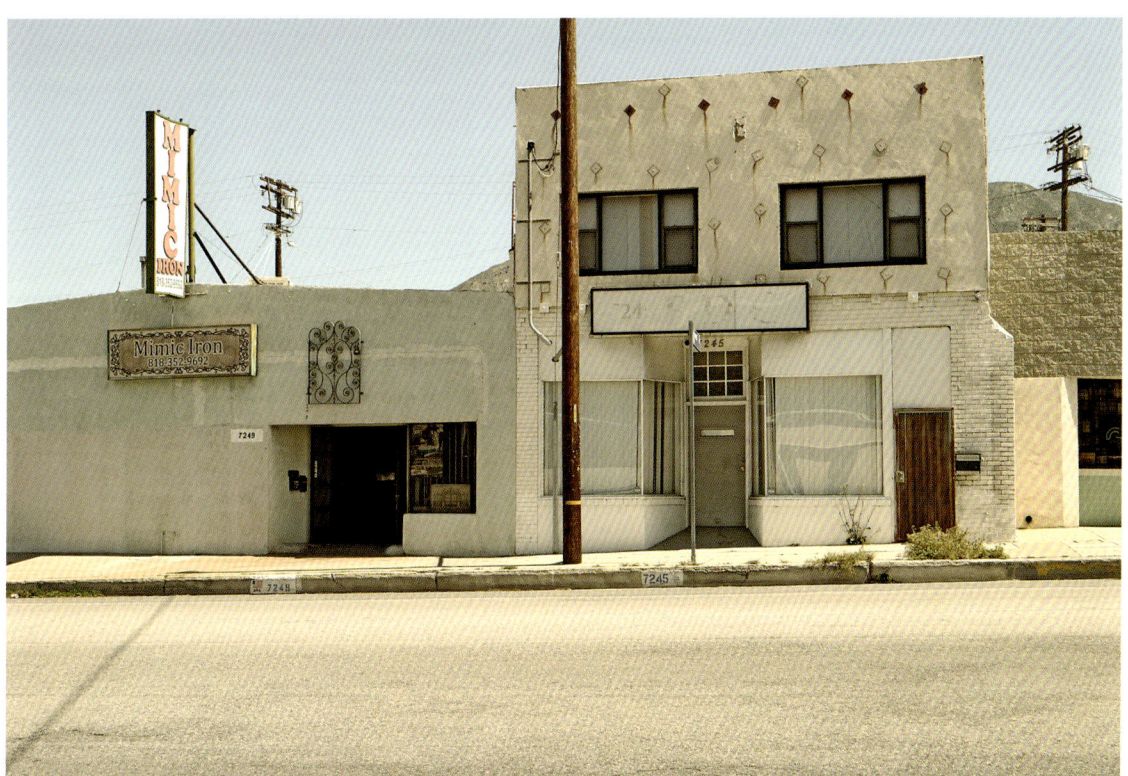

Stapleton, Colorado

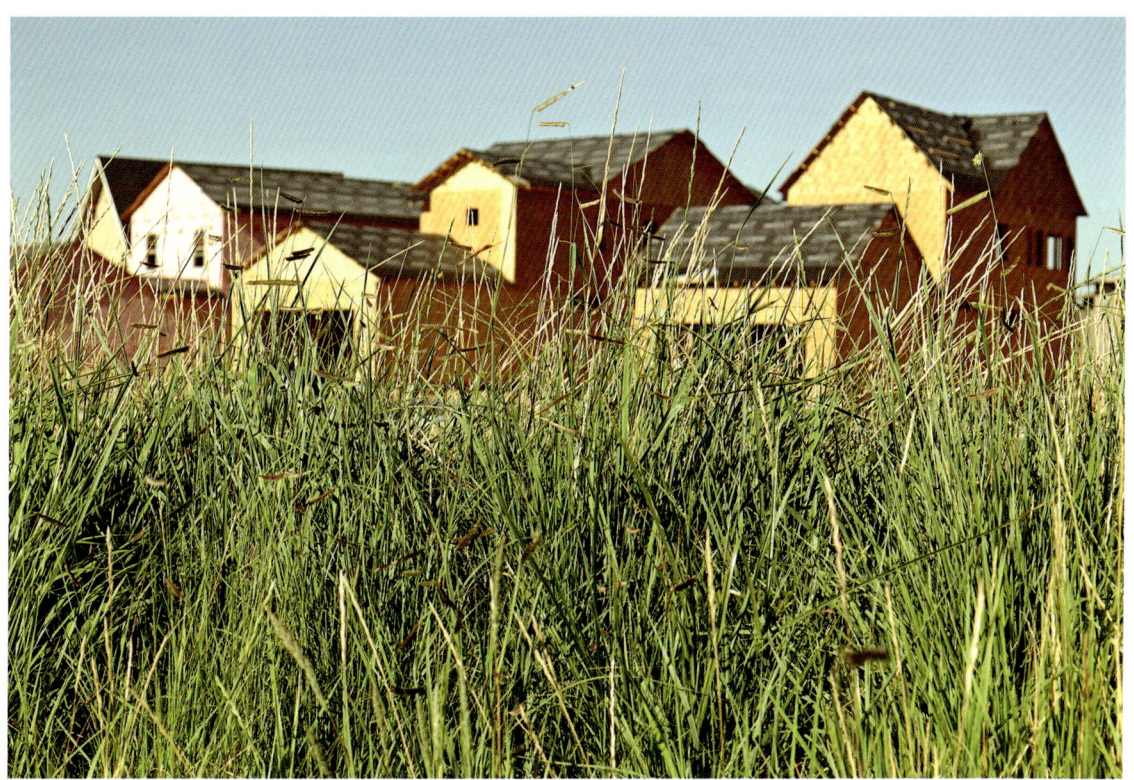

Las Vegas, Nevada

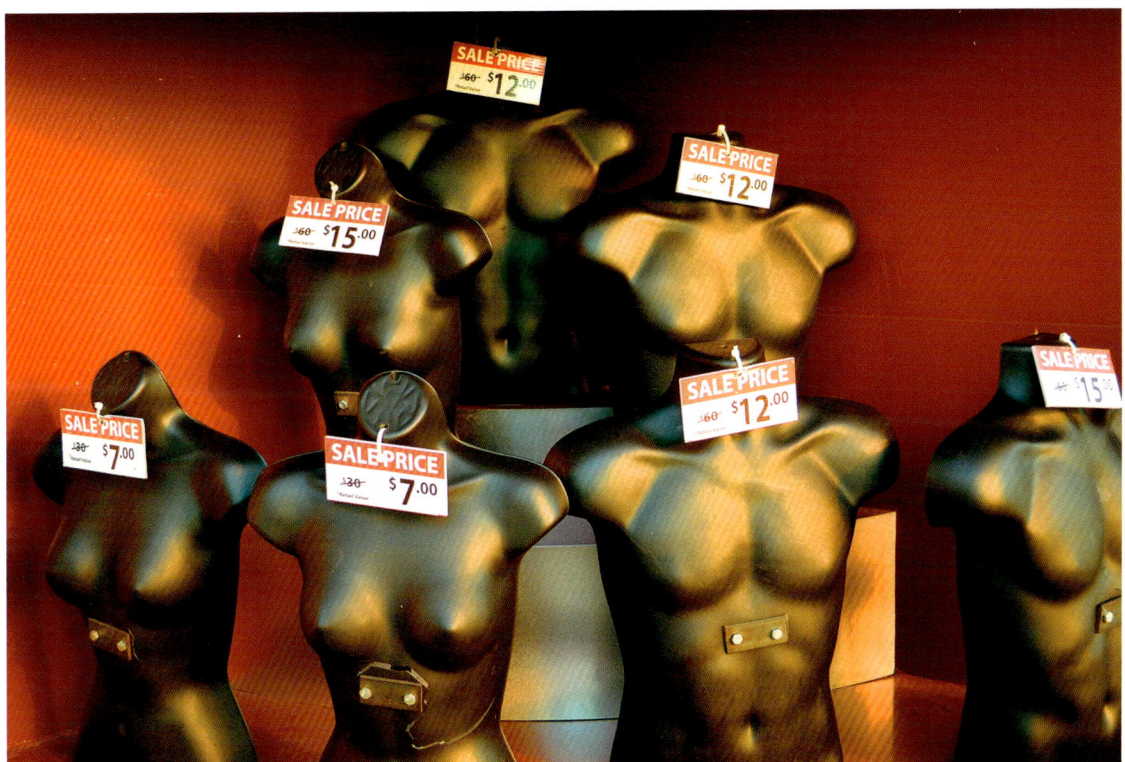

Fresno, California

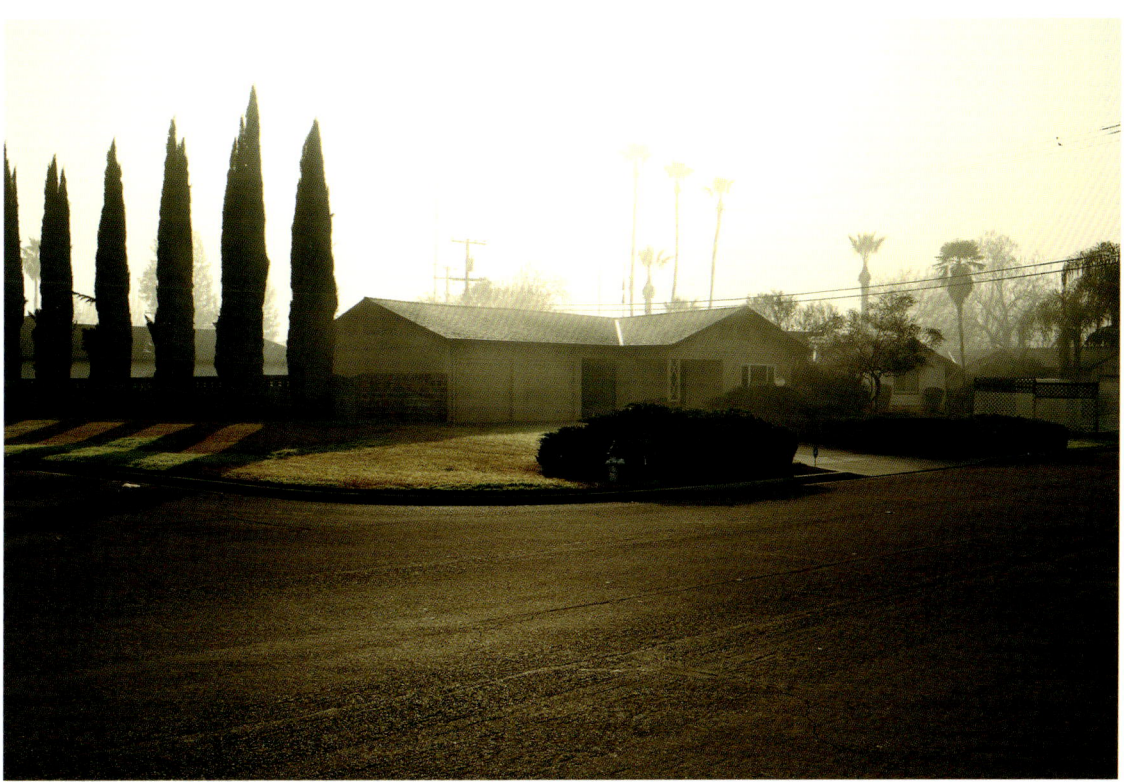

Venice, California

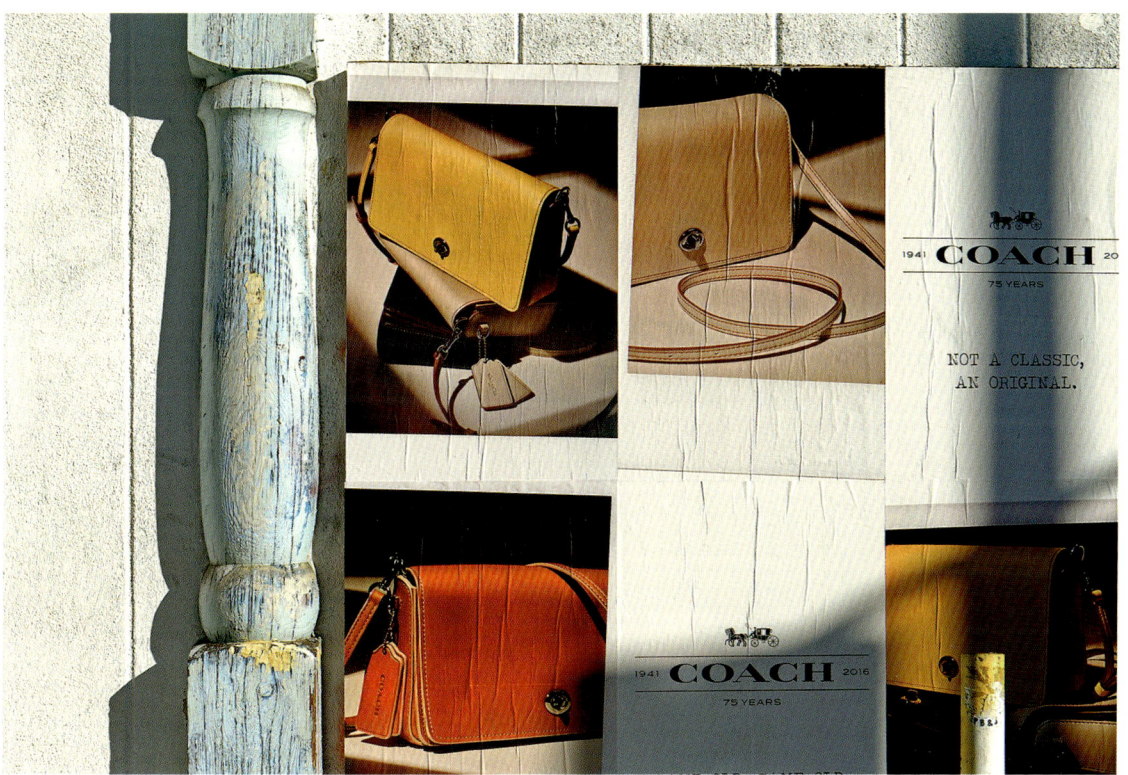

Gallup, New Mexico

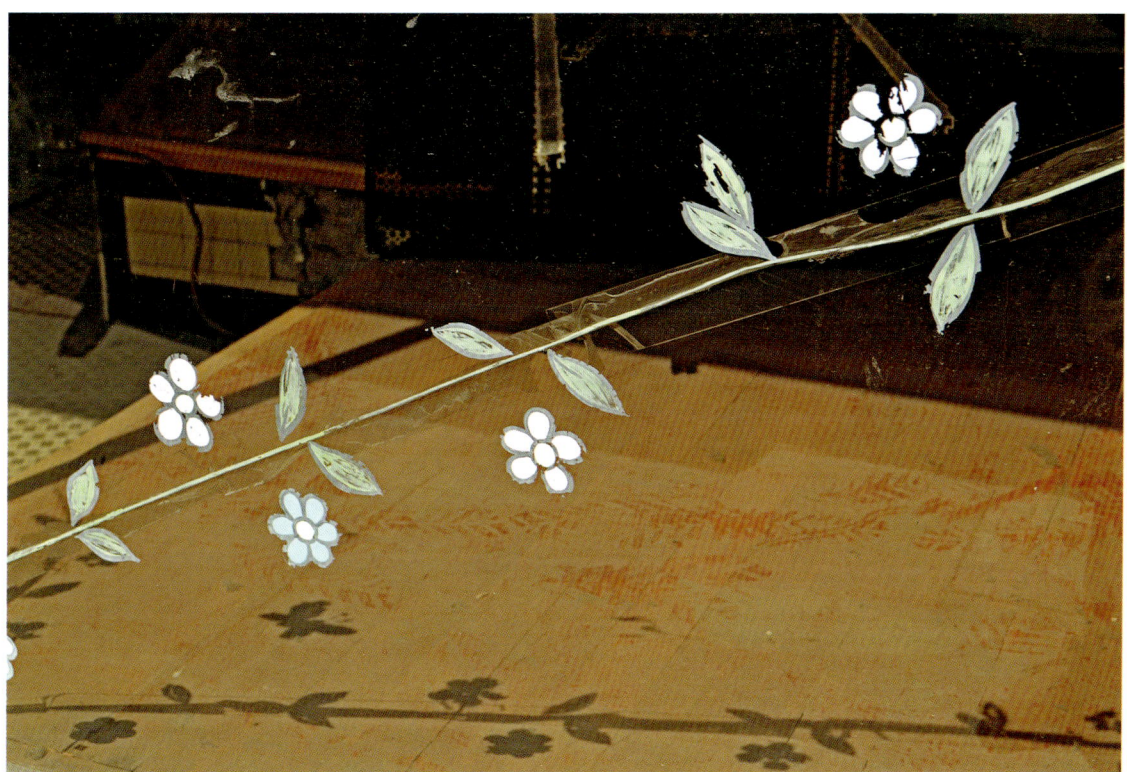

Santa Monica, California

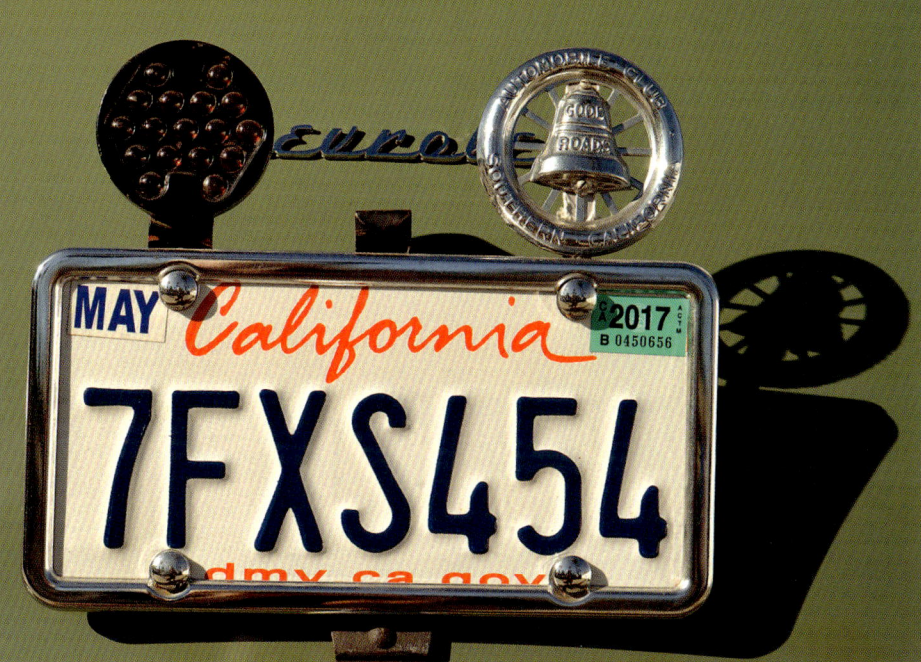

Flagstaff, Arizona

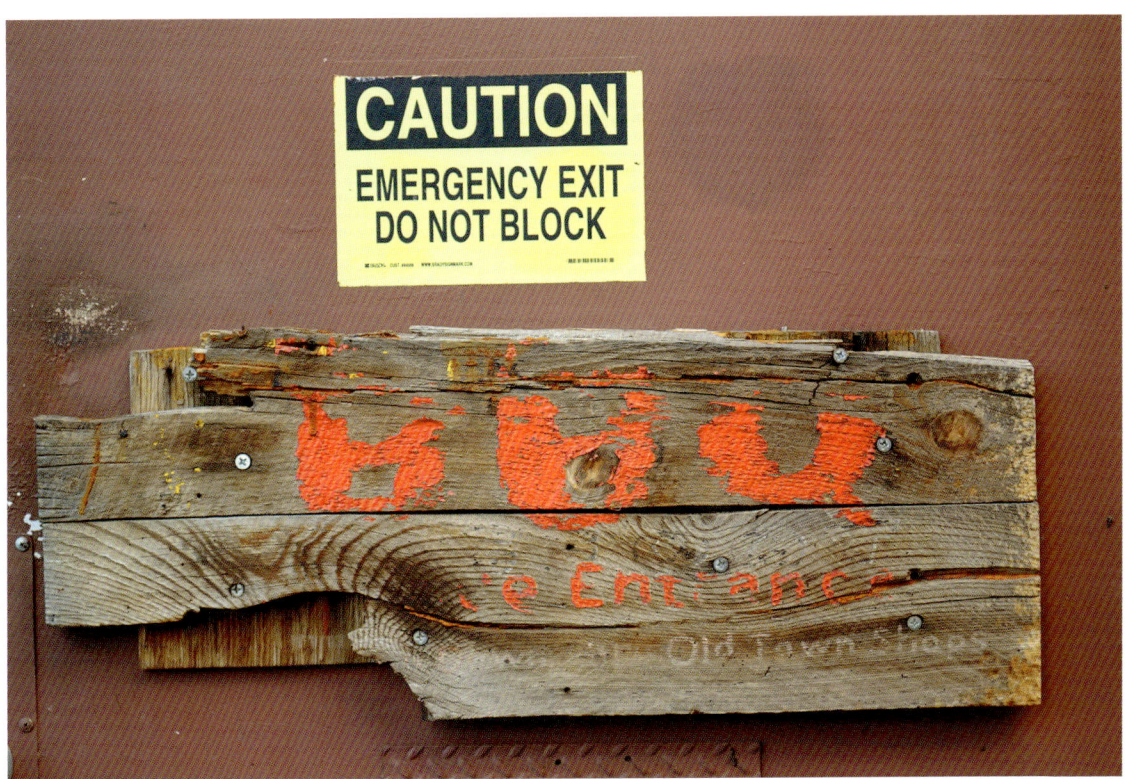

San Pedro, California

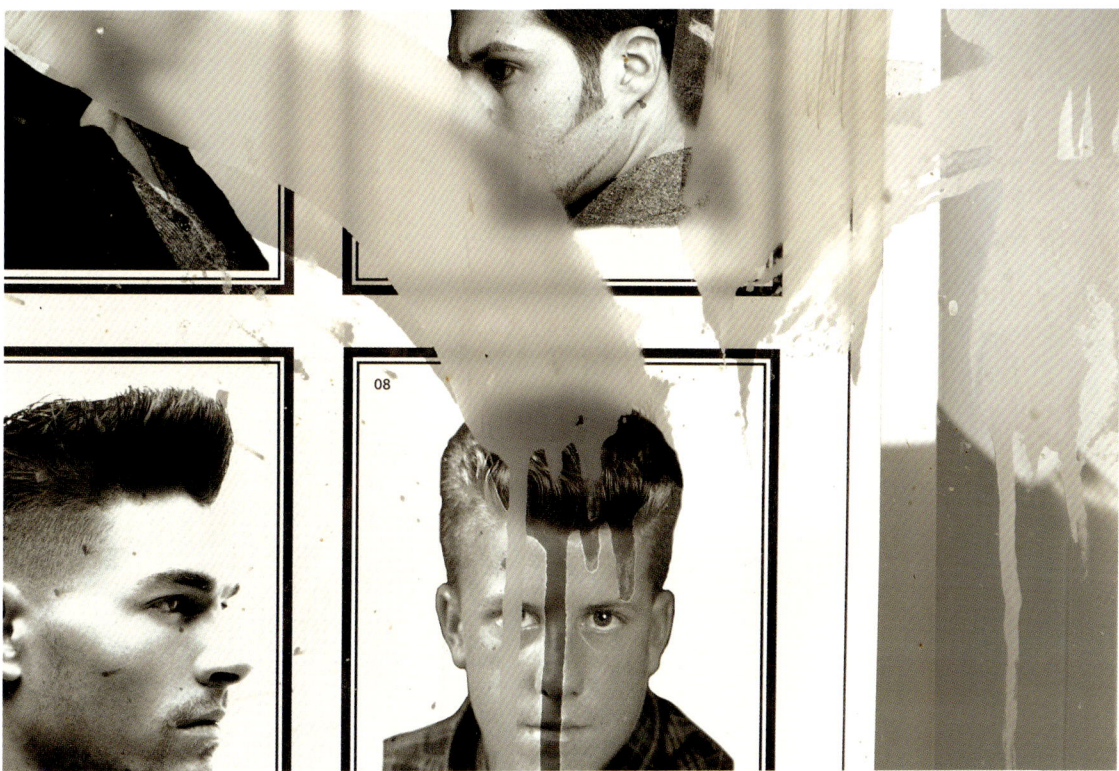

08

Seligman, Arizona

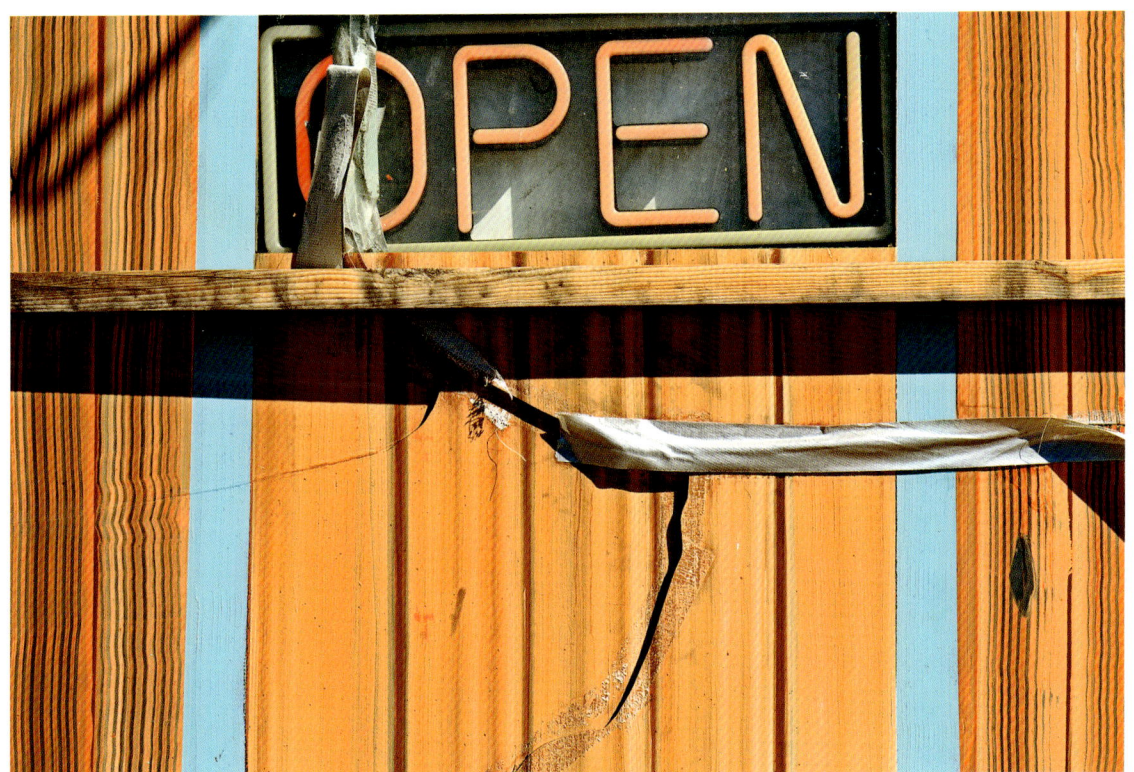

St. Joseph, Missouri

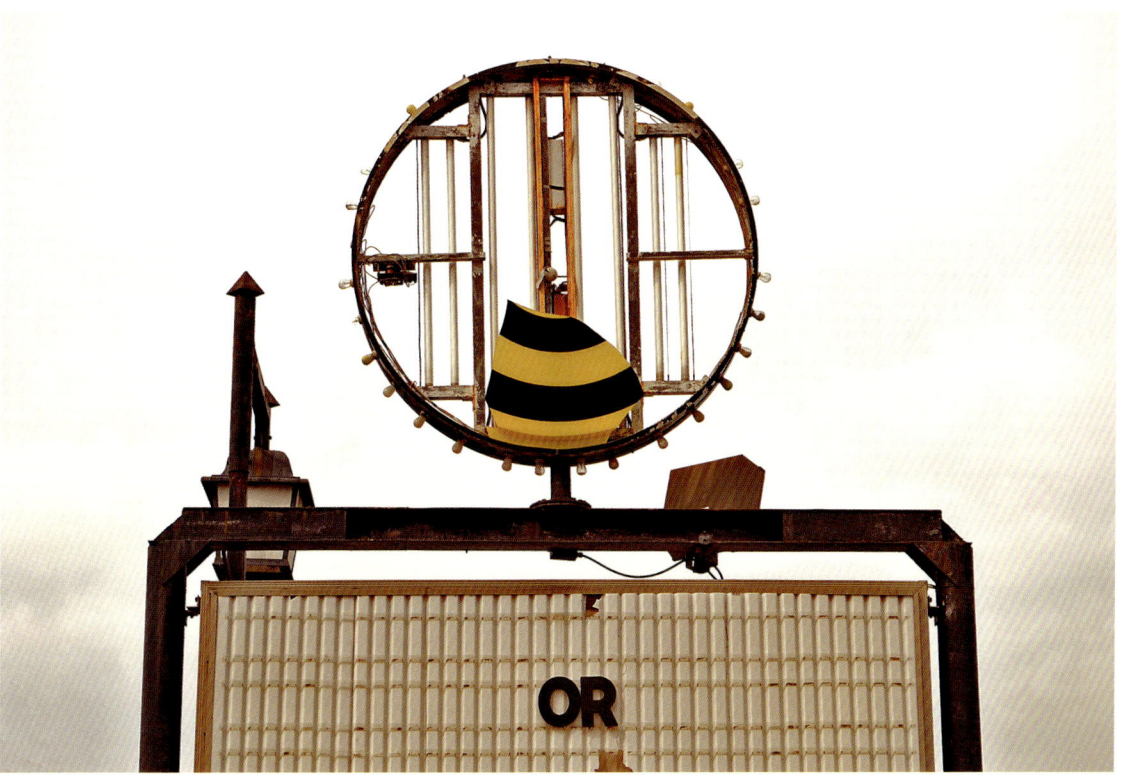

Springfield, Illinois

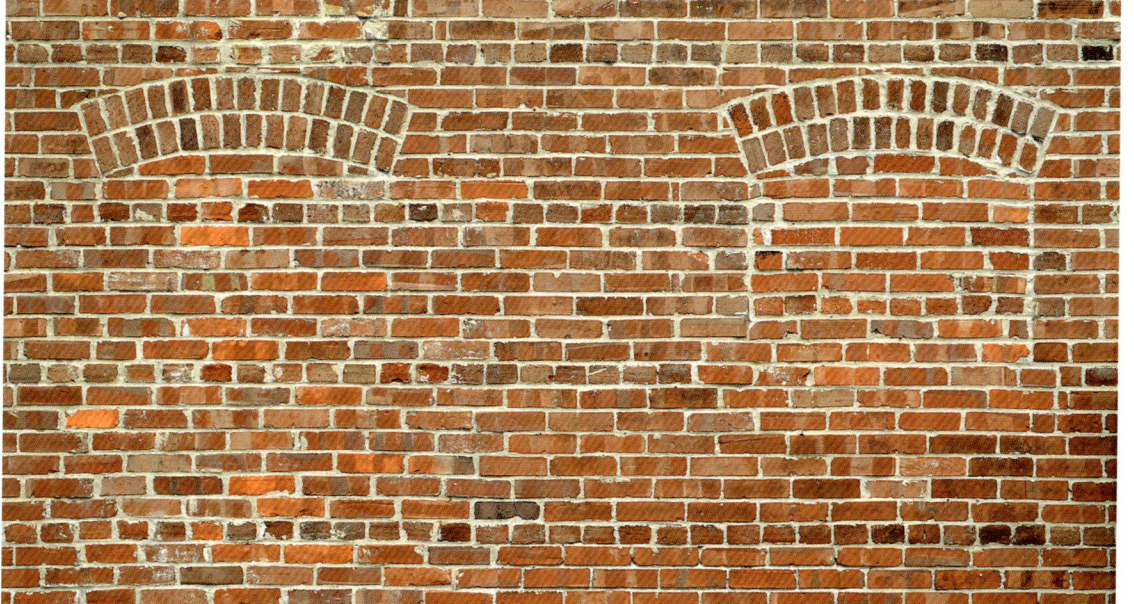

Toledo, Ohio

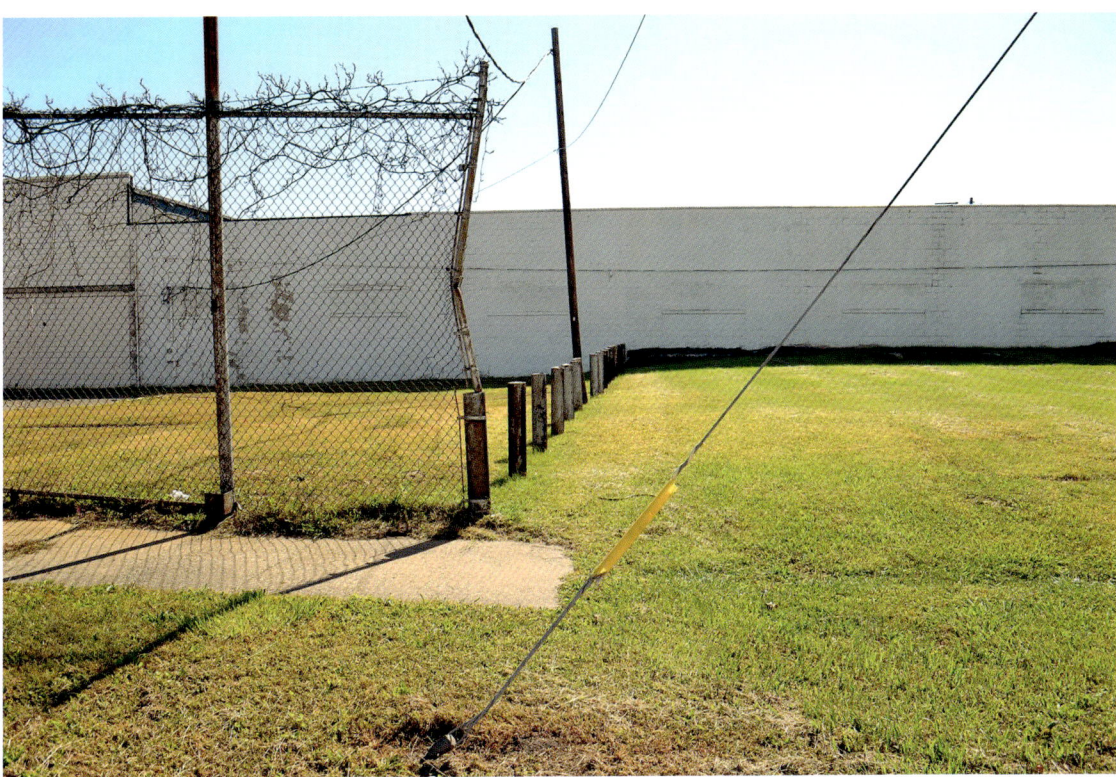

Cleveland, Ohio

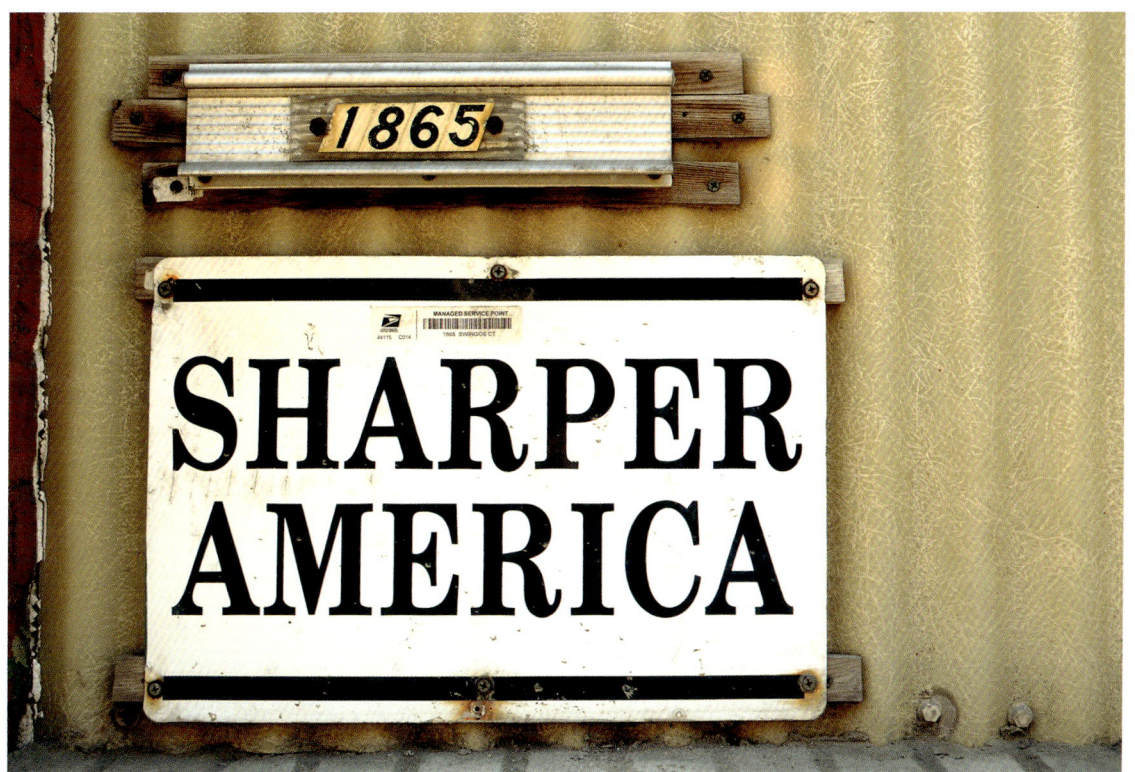

San Onofre, California

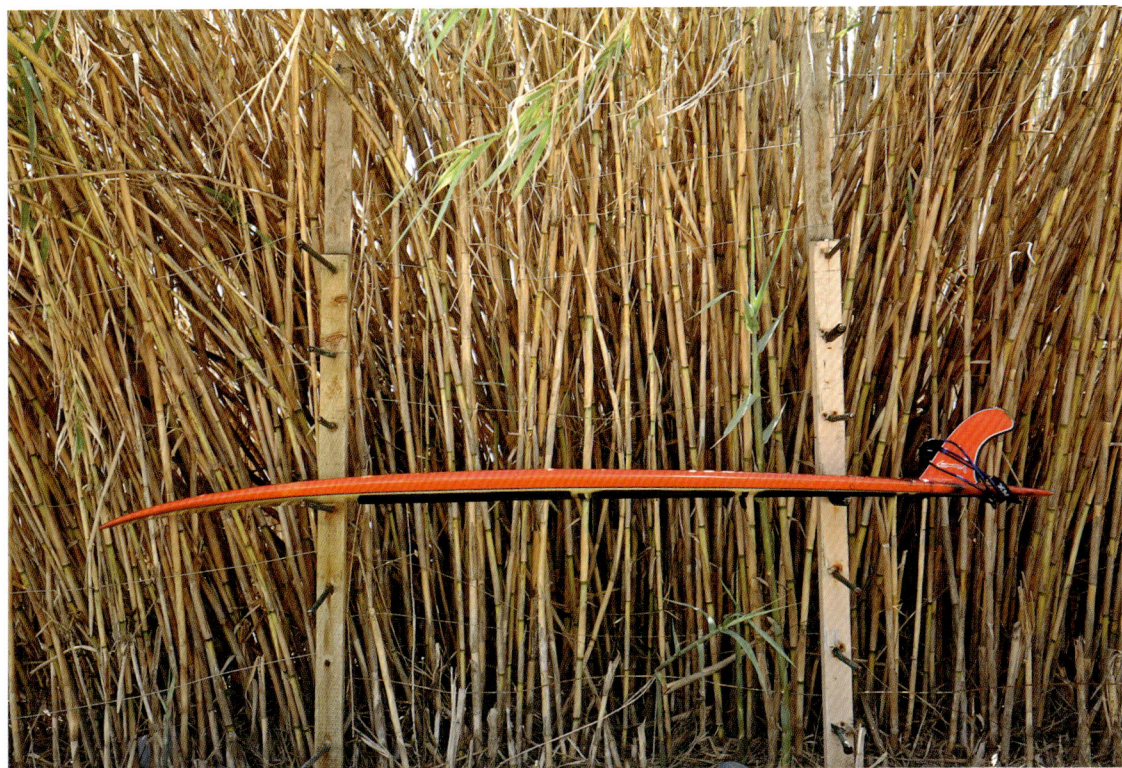

Antonito, Colorado

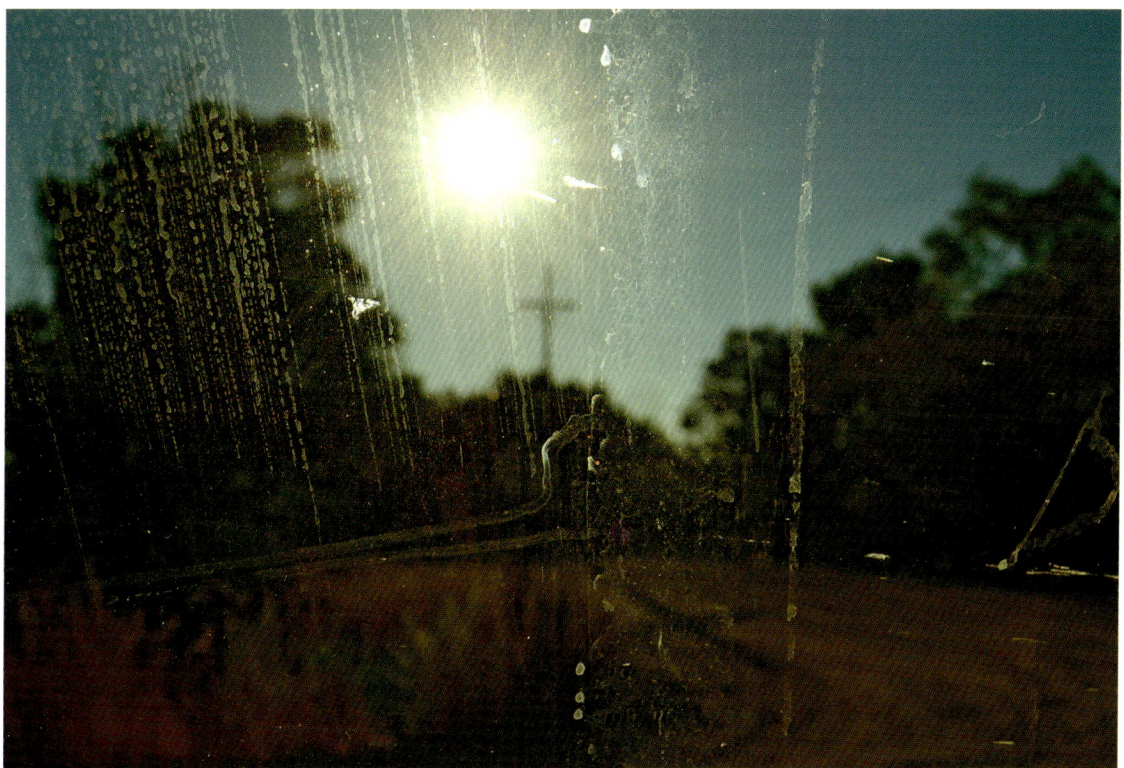

San Benito County, California

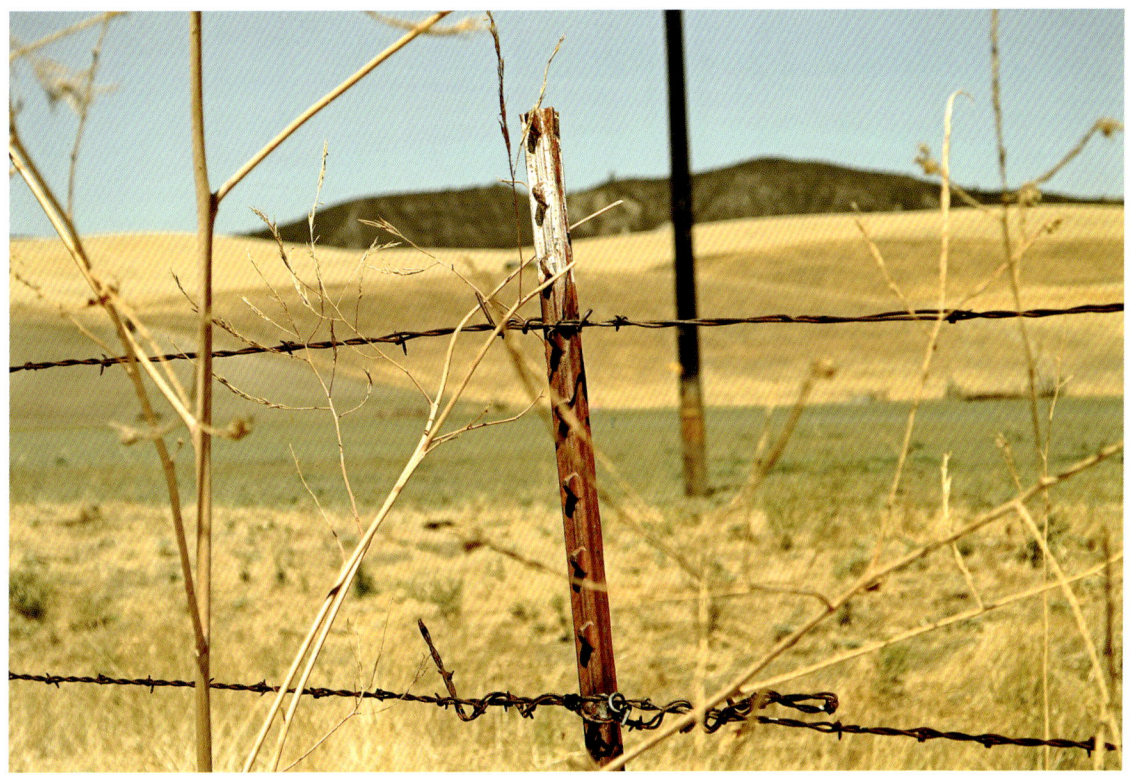

Chicago, Illinois

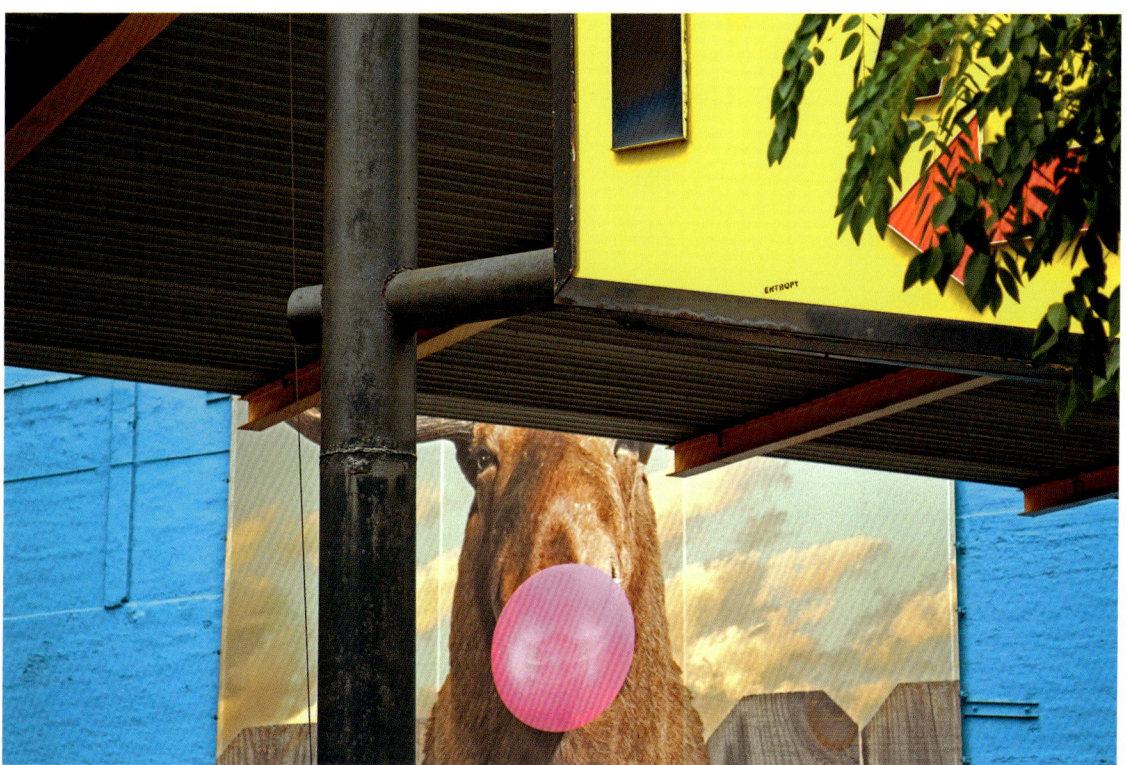

San Pedro, California

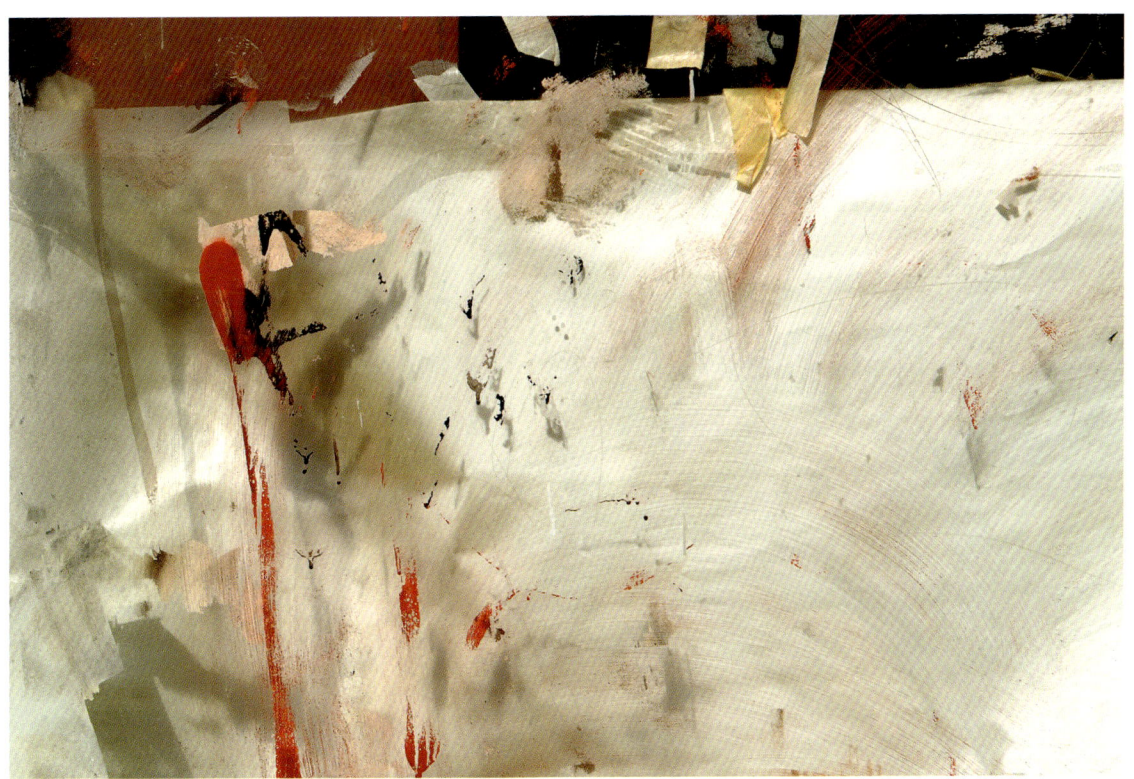

Kingman, Arizona

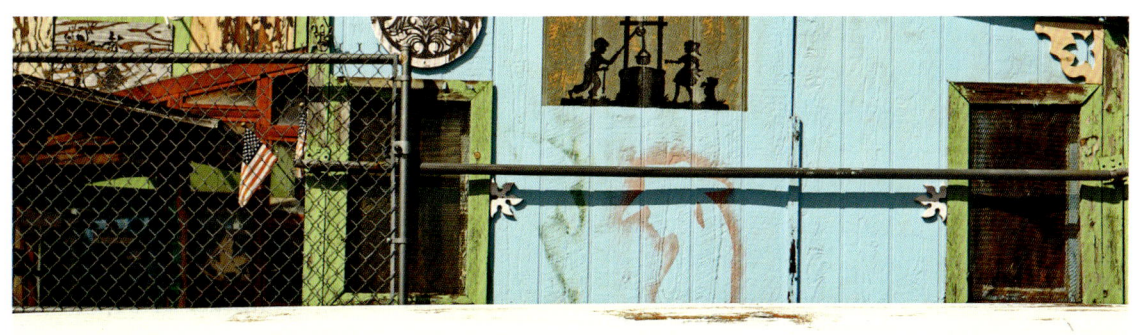

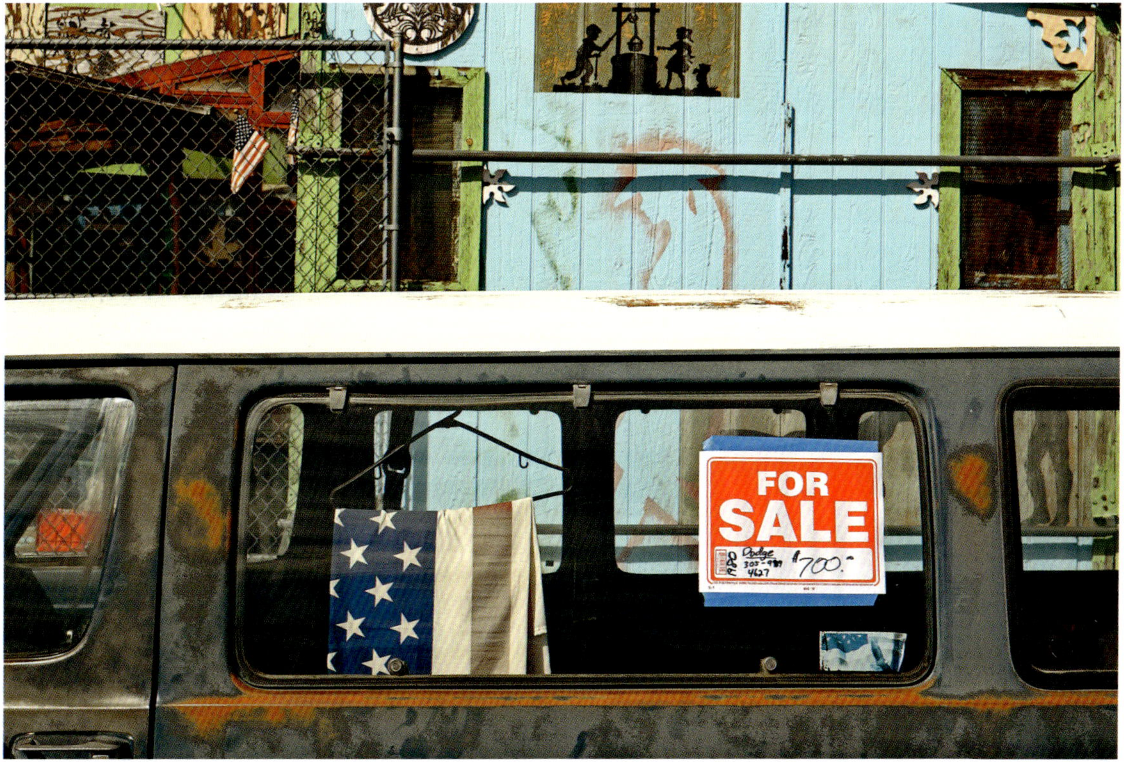

Flagstaff, Arizona

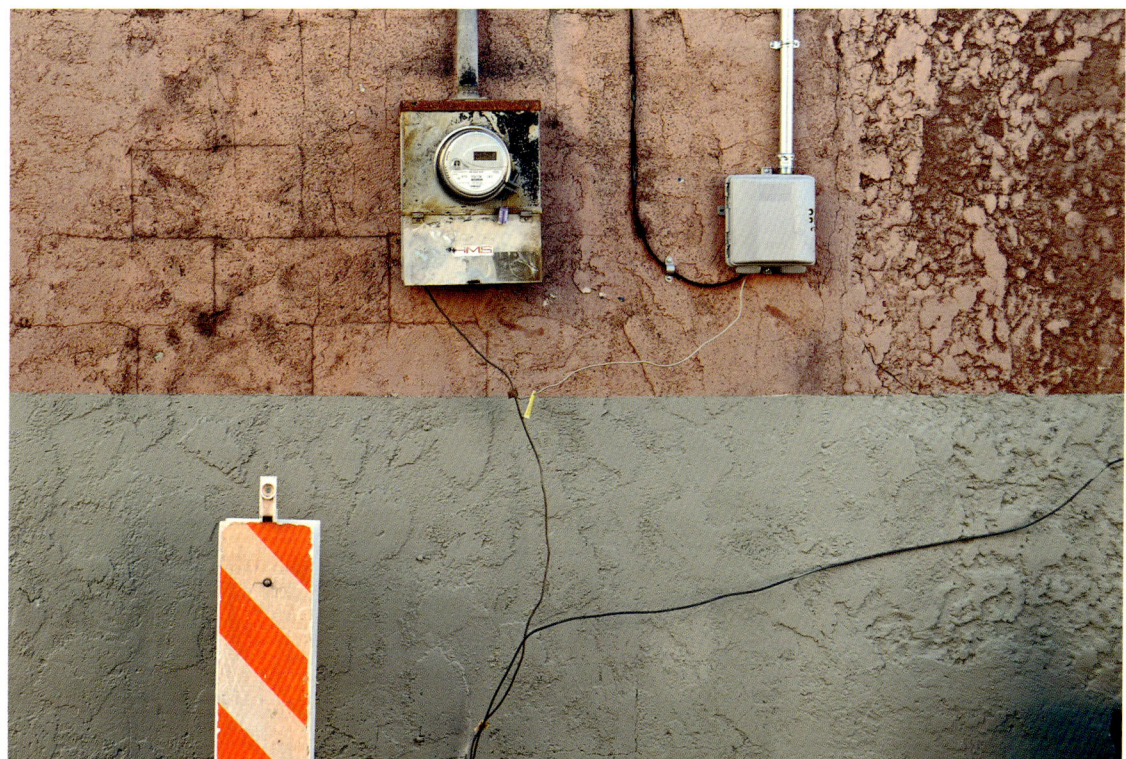

244   Royal Gorge, Colorado

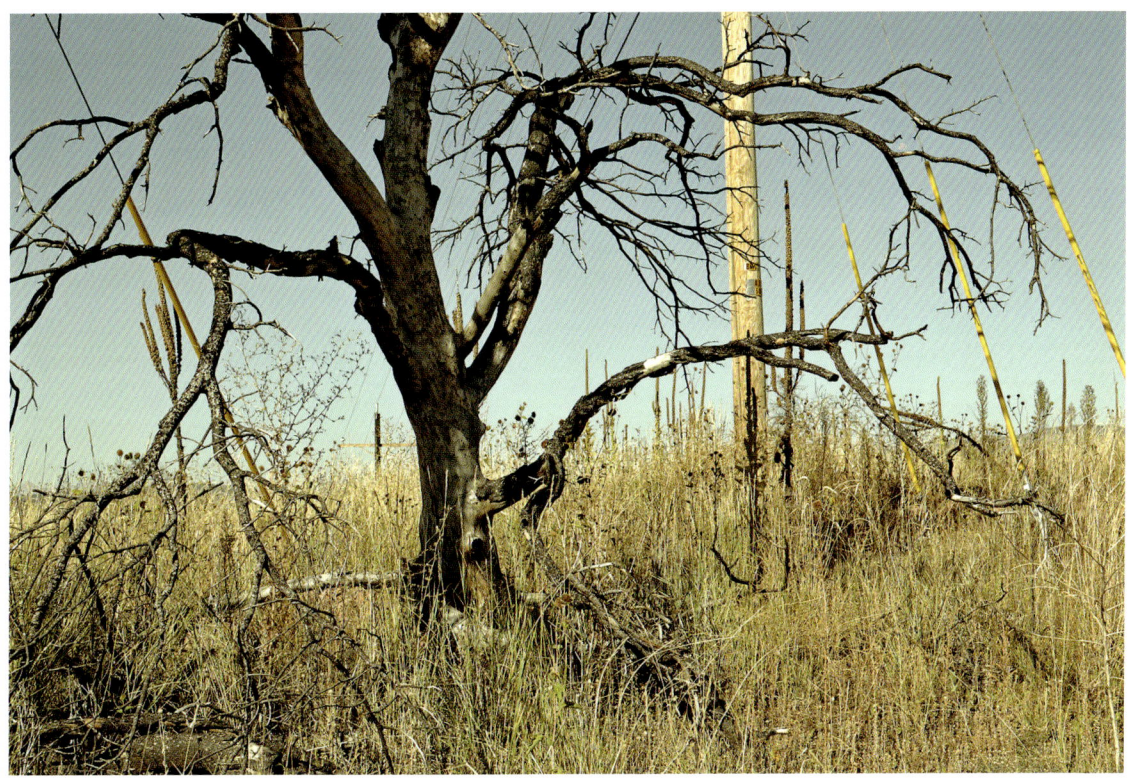

Cabazon, California

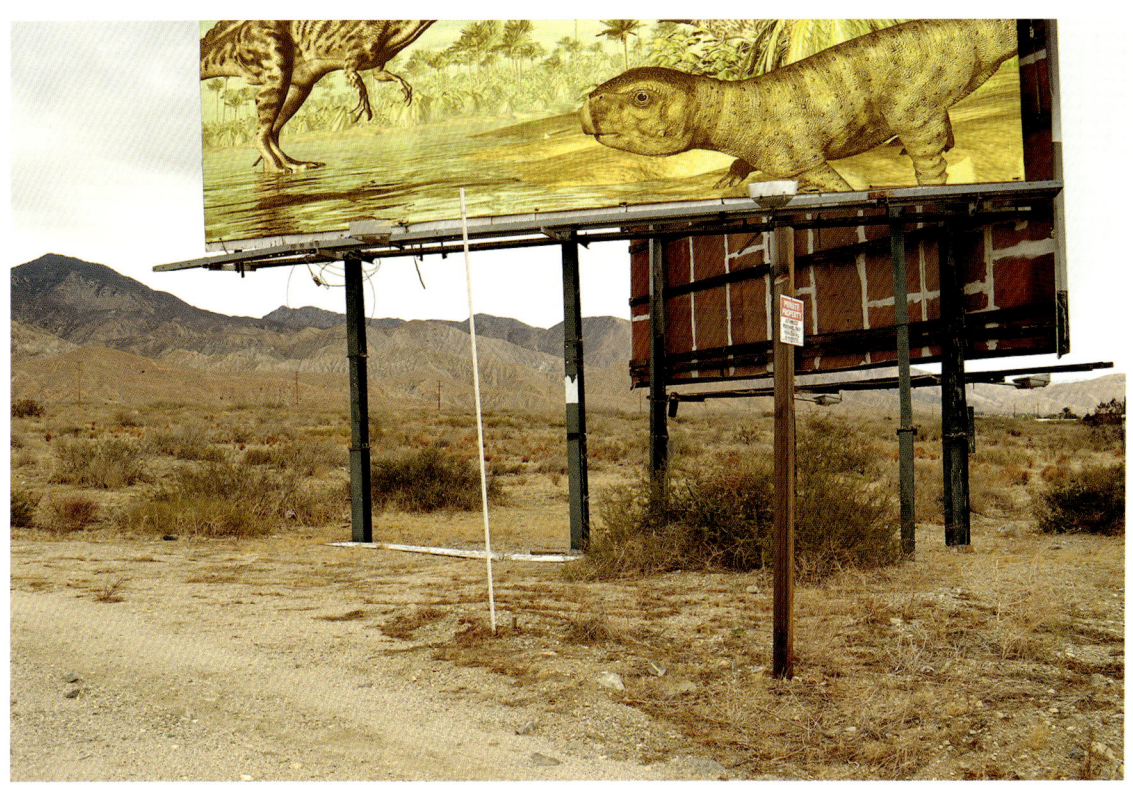

Normal, Illinois

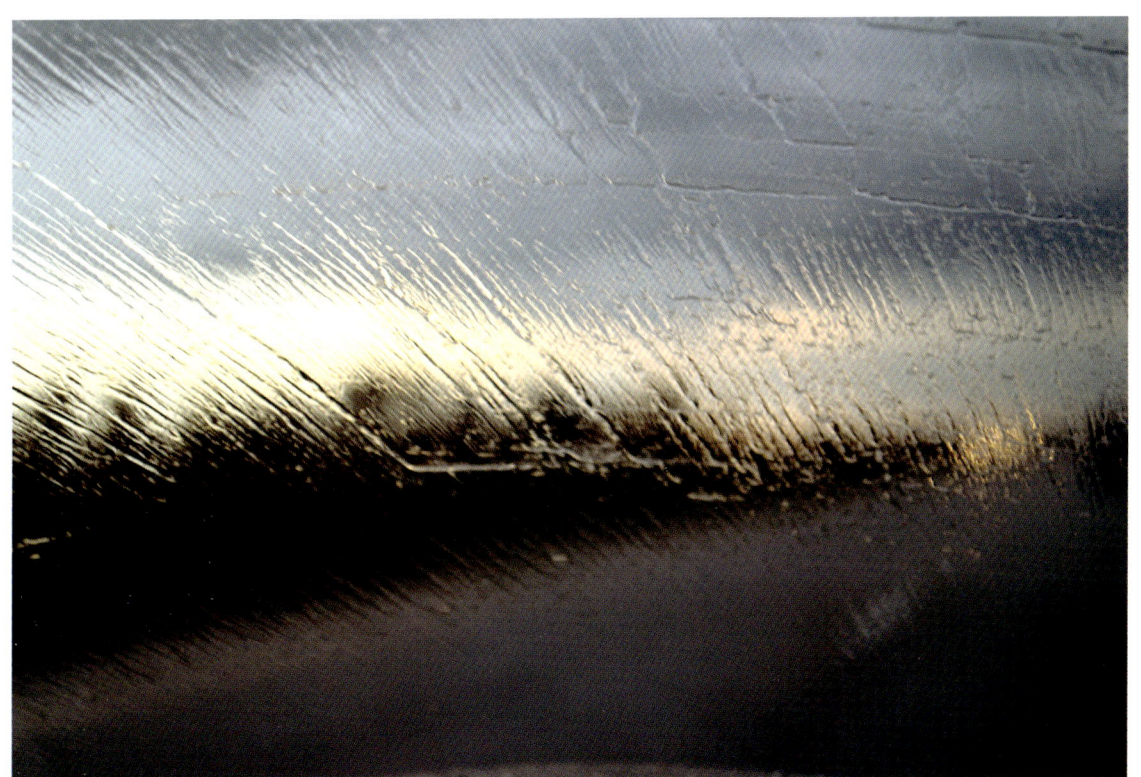

Astoria, New York

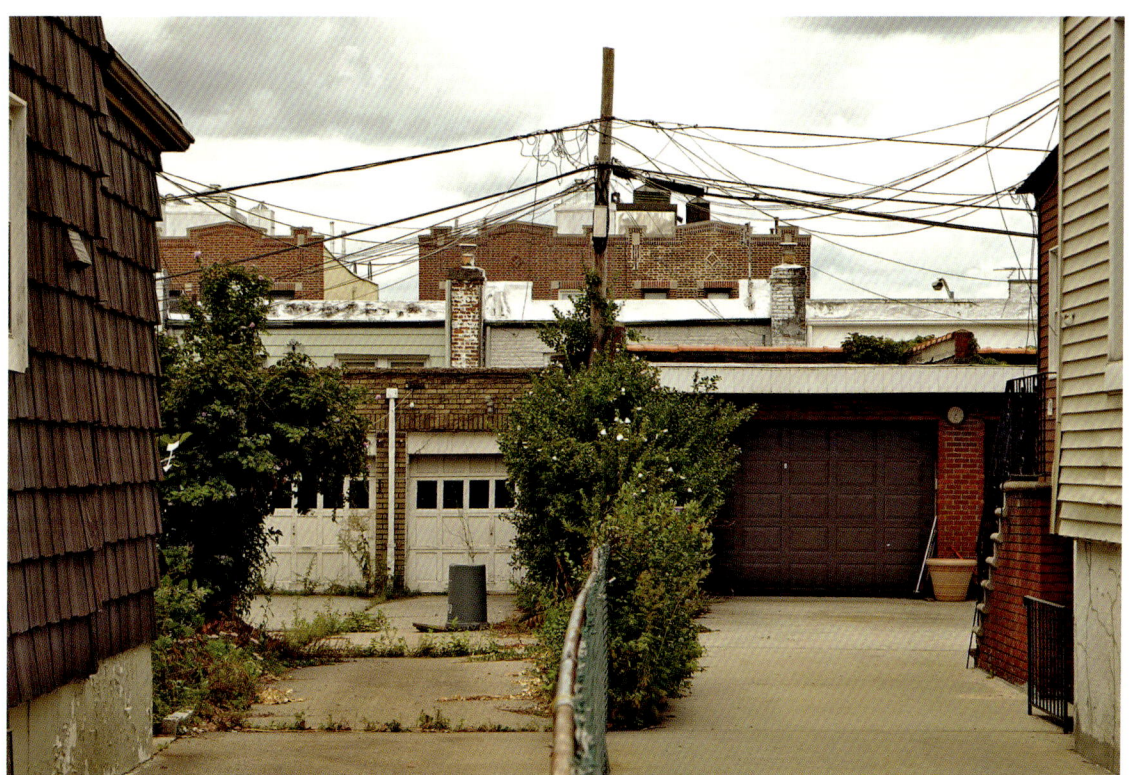

Harmony, California

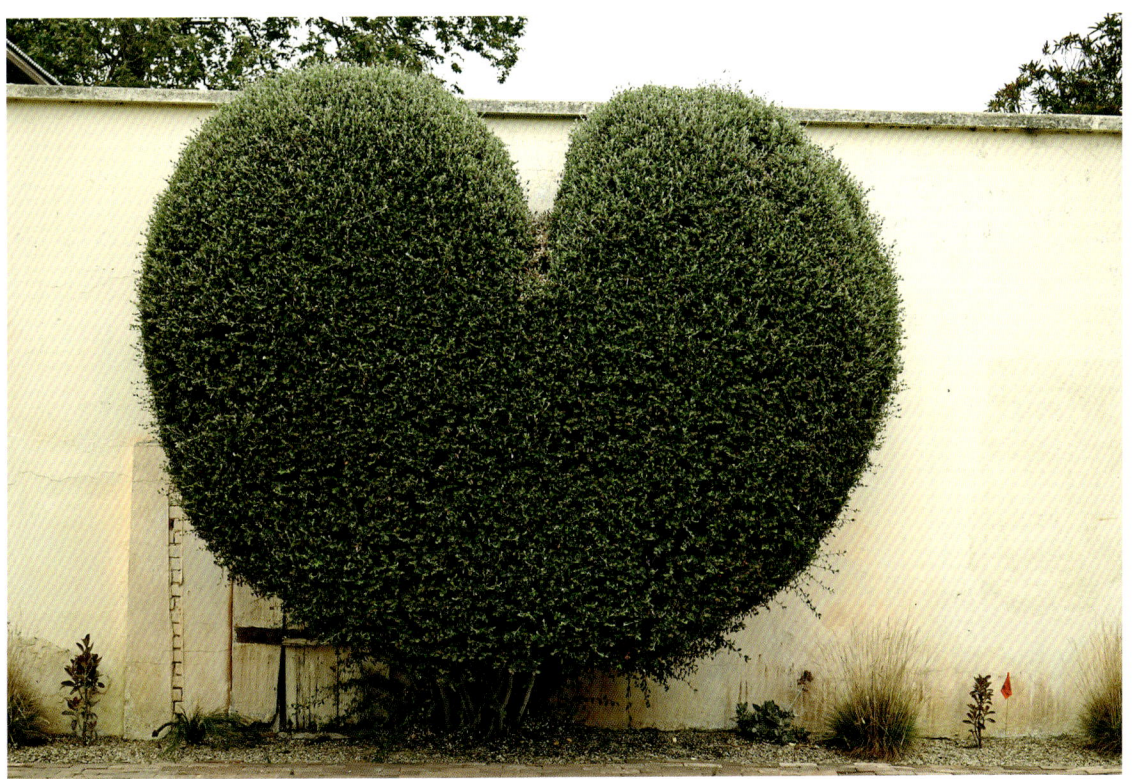

Gingko Press, Inc.
1321 Fifth Street
Berkeley, CA 94710, USA
www.gingkopress.com

First published in the United States of America, May 2017.
First Edition, 1000 copies
Copyright © 2017 Rudy VanderLans
ISBN: 978-1-58423-653-5

Printed in China.
Book design by Rudy VanderLans.
Typeset in Alda, designed by Berton Hasebe.

Once again, many thanks to Mo Cohen and David Lopes at Gingko Press, and to my wife Zuzana Licko.

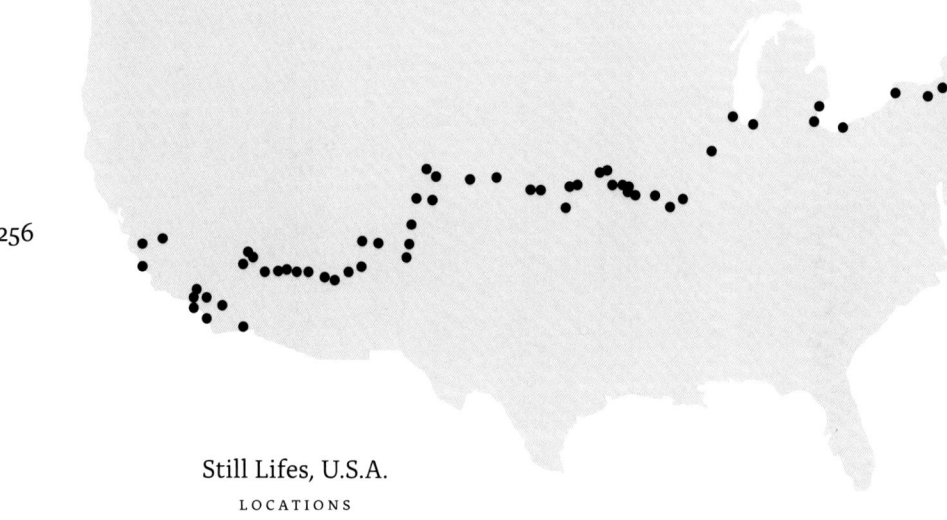

Still Lifes, U.S.A.

LOCATIONS

SCALE   0   150   300   450   600   750   900   1050   MILES

2015 ~ 2016